Business Model Innova[t]

Based on the author's 30 years of consulting experience and validated by doctoral research, this book focuses on creating profitable growth with business model innovation in medium and large companies.

Arising from an increased need for systems thinking and technological development, there is a common understanding that a business model should primarily create, develop, and retain value for companies' customers. But increased globalization and resource constraints have led to a difficult balancing act when addressing the challenges of achieving profitable processes and long-term growth. This book provides a new framework, based on six central themes with five related success factors each, to enhance opportunities' visibility, contribute to improved margins, increase awareness of a company's unique strengths and weaknesses in overall resources, manage risk, and optimize implementation of a new model throughout an entire organization.

Owners, board members, and managers of medium and large companies worldwide, as well as advanced business students, will appreciate this detailed, practical, and clarifying approach to business model innovation.

Dr. Staffan Hedén has a long successful career as a business leader, consultant, and academic. For the past 30 years, he has been fully focusing on understanding and developing expert knowledge that contributes to healthy and profitable growth in medium and large companies, especially companies operating in several international markets. The knowledge that has been developed focuses on clarifying what strategies are required, understanding bottlenecks, using resources better, and being able to visualize unique abilities. At the core, it is about understanding how individuals best create performance and how different groups value loyalty. Dr. Hedén has been working with over 150 international groups of companies (in whole, parts or as a mentor), conducted more than 3,000 interviews focusing on business model innovation, and created over 1,500 seminars in the field.

Business Model Innovation

How it really works

Dr. Staffan Hedén

Routledge
Taylor & Francis Group

NEW YORK AND LONDON

Designed cover image: Getty

First published 2024
by Routledge
605 Third Avenue, New York, NY 10158

and by Routledge
4 Park Square, Milton Park, Abingdon, Oxon, OX14 4RN

Routledge is an imprint of the Taylor & Francis Group, an informa business

ISBN: 978-1-032-51415-4 (hbk)
ISBN: 978-1-032-51414-7 (pbk)
ISBN: 978-1-003-40212-1 (ebk)

DOI: 10.4324/9781003402121

Typeset in Optima
by Apex CoVantage, LLC

This work is dedicated to all of the customers, past, present, and future who are supported by its findings and conclusions.

To my amazing wife Hanna who supports me in all ways of my life and in this work.

To all my eight beautiful children you are always with me.

Contents

Preface   *viii*

Acknowledgments   *ix*

1 Introduction   1

2 Strategy   12

3 Existing business model   34

4 Customer orientation   56

5 Management   78

6 Organizational structure   101

7 Resources   124

8 Summary   148

Index   *176*

Preface

As I sit at my laptop at the end of the journey of writing my first book, I feel the joy and anticipation that has characterized my life every day for the past five years; I fulfilled my dreams by working hard through my career before going on to complete my doctorate at the University of Warwick – Warwick Business School as a practitioner with a solid bank of experiences. Then I had the opportunity of being a guest professor using my expertise in business model innovation and now I have written a book – after about three decades as a business consultant for international companies – a writing process of almost four months in solitude but with long walks and my own thoughts. The focus that these experiences have given me has allowed me to reflect on all the extraordinary people and companies I have had the privilege to encounter along the way. As I stepped into the world of work all those years ago, I could never have imagined having so many exciting and fulfilling opportunities.

It has truly been a voyage of discovery for me through my work as a founder, business manager, and business consultant, and through continued work and application through academia, I have seen the value of this new framework in business model innovation in both the real world and how it impacts those who study this field. My aim in creating this book is to be able to reach out to the leadership of these organizations to show that creating projects of innovation is not just something that is done once but is a constantly evolving adventure that can expand your expectations of what your company and team are capable of.

I hope that this book will provide a great benefit for you as a professional in the field of business and that it will contribute to your knowledge about how it is possible to develop existing business models by using business model innovation and the framework within this book.

Acknowledgments

There are many people who have contributed to my work as an action researcher and been involved over time who have contributed to more knowledge indirectly and directly. My previous work has focused on research, consulting, and management, and it has been an important piece of the puzzle, which I am only really reflecting on now. It would be impossible to count every individual who I have had contact with through my career in working with business model innovation; it has literally been a cast of thousands that have given their voices and insights to this work. To all the customers, leaders, managers, workers, researchers, interviewees, and everyone who gave their time and energy, you know who are and you have my deepest thanks. This could not have been done without you.

My journey has been filled with mentors, researchers, and academic supervisors and colleagues who have given me support and space to develop my work with applied research with international companies. Thank you all for the gifts of your insights, dedication, and strong foundation so that I could grow. I would especially like to thank Associate Professor Sikander Khan for a great collaboration and that you always give me your full support in my ambition to learn new things. In addition, to Annika Adebäck, Lic. Psychotherapist and Psychoanalyst IPA, for giving me invaluable support that created new bridges and contributed to new paths. Of course, also to my supervisor in connection with my doctorate Christian Stadler, Professor of Strategic Management, who made me deepen and develop my knowledge in business model innovation, an absolutely invaluable help with questions and conversations. Thanks also for important conversations, development issues in contributions to : Professor Tina Keifer, Professor Kurt Matzler and Professor James Hayton. Finally, Assistant Professor Peter Ek, for long talks about different viewpoints and helping me to sort my thoughts.

The most central people for the book's creation are my Editor/Researcher Melanie Boyd in Edinburgh, Senior Advisor/Researcher Hanna Lindsäter Hedén, and our Financial Officer Rolf Åman. I lack words for how to describe Melanie; her commitment, professionalism, and her clear-sighted conclusions. Thank you, Melanie. Thanks also to Hanna for your unique ability to analyze, balance, and see opportunities along the journey of the creation of this book. This work could not have been done without you being my partner, colleague, and best friend, I love you. Rolf, who has been with me for all of these almost 30 years, has been absolutely invaluable to me not only as a businessman and consultant but also as a friend who has listened to various stories. Thanks Rolf for an amazing collaboration. Finally, a big thank you to Art Director Ira Hörling Rudal who helped me to create simplification and order in the book's images.

Chapter 1

Introduction

The last 25 years with a focus on business model innovation

I have been working with action research from the mid-1990s with an aim toward accelerating businesses with business model innovation. This book is a result of my overall experience and work with over 150 medium and large business customers since I founded Cecia Consulting in 1996.[1] I started to work with clients' management problems directly as they had good strategies but needed help to develop them. Several of the early customers also wanted help to develop structures and their organizations, which led to several seminars.

Early on, I focused on using customers' own resources to build more knowledge in place, develop solutions for customers, including deliveries and solving bottlenecks along the way. Gradually, my customers became medium and large groups, usually with direct contact and work with the owner, board, group CEO, or C-suites in subsidiaries. I developed knowledge of how my company could create results through active intervention. It has been a mix of local Scandinavian groups, groups with a focus in Europe, and over half of the customers have been global international groups with a focus on many markets at the same time.

I have always worked closely together with a leader from the organization to solve questions with different research techniques and usually with a combination of conversations, qualitative studies, quantitative studies, and focus groups. This has meant that my method has been able to develop step by step, and it has contributed to completely unexpected results and been incredibly effective. The method is practically designed, logical, and easy to communicate and follow as a tool for medium and large companies when it is time to implement an innovation process of their business model. In all historical contacts with customers, industry colleagues, and academia, the method has emerged which is completely unique.

In this chapter I will start by providing you, the reader, with an insight into the framework developed from my customers' experience and in the

DOI: 10.4324/9781003402121-1

last chapter of the book, you will find a summary of how to use the concepts. Within the body of this book, you will find an overview of business model and business model innovation, the advent of the themes and success factors and selected cases, including research and follow-ups. The structure in Chapters 2 to 7 focuses on six different themes, presented with five subheadings, and each subheading then has three stories from real cases that I worked with as a consultant and support the reasoning behind these subheadings. These stories (italicized parts of the book from Chapters 2 to 7) are descriptions of the company, what issues were at play, how the issues were addressed, and what the outcome was. Within each success factor, there are five insights, which head the section to make it easy to follow the evolution of the insights through the section. Each section then ends with a summary to bring all of these individual pieces together.

Within each theme through the book, I consistently use "us" and "we," meaning me, the employees, the customers, and possibly others who have been with us in groups in various projects. By using these terms, it pays tribute to the clients and team who have helped me develop my knowledge through the years and to make it clear that it has been a group effort. The six different themes also have five main areas built into the texts: the global world, change, technology, drive/signal development, and future. These areas also have analogies that can explain them more deeply and with additional perspective.

The thing that is important to understand before this journey begins is that the key word in developing existing business models is *adventure*. While the goal and anticipated outcome is growth and positive change, it has to be acknowledged that as with any adventure there are inherent risks and perils along the way. The road ahead is not always smooth, there are often obstacles in the way, and some days it may seem like it would have just been easier to stay at home and do things as they've always been done. However, it is also true that when risks are taken and perseverance is shown that there are great outcomes for those who dare to try. Change is a challenge, but in taking on the challenge, in my experience, the rewards can be incredible.

How it really works

For me, this process of making a book has added new dimensions to this work with companies as an action researcher. The whole new developed framework creates fantastic opportunities for medium and large companies to build a safer and more profitable innovation process by using these themes, success factors, and insights to strengthen the existing company in a business model innovation project.

The outcome is a creation of six themes, 30 factors and 150 insights and, when used with experiences, a GUIDE and an ATLAS. The different themes are strategy, existing business model, customer orientation, management, organizational structure, and resources. The six themes can build a platform to clarify the company's unique success factors. The 30 success factors in total are used as a mirror when the projects are continued from the drawing table to the implementation. It is not decisive whether the project concerns an entire company, parts of a company, or a product development.

The book will give a wider opportunity for a successful business innovation process and by using the map as a mirror when undergoing a change in your business format. It is a great advantage to be able to manage a process with a framework that can also act preventively and be able to cover a larger area from what creates the business, how it delivers value, how collaborations are built, how the structure and organization deliver against customer needs, and how the models look forward with relevant key resources to compete better.

The GUIDE

Each one of the six themes has five success factors that are described in more detail in Chapters 2 to 7 – where all 30 success factors have their own names. The GUIDE is an opportunity to see the different themes laid out and how the factors can connect to those themes in an organized way.

GUIDE

Themes and factors

	Strategy	Existing BM	Customer orientation	Management	Organizational structure	Resource
Factors	Before	Evaluate	Energize	New situation	Security and support	Review
	Anchoring	Time	Management structure	Clarify BM	Anchored with leaders	Reinforce
	Simplify	Anchoring	Increase knowledge	Open and present	Variables for speed	Hidden values
	Load-bearing	Value	Opportunity	Lead through others	The process	Building innovations
	Living	Follow-ups	Margin and deliveries	Three-Step Management	Decision support	Implementation

Figure 1.1 A perspective of the factors within each theme of Business Model Innovation.

However, it is not necessary for every innovation case to use all of these factors, and in each success factor, there are then five insights, which allow for a deepening of each theme with questions. This acts as a guide to target the path forward through a change, creating a framework to create your very own atlas for the journey ahead.

The GUIDE can act as an extra engine when the wind is not blowing on the sea when you are in your sailboat and you can still choose the speed and destination. It can also act as a catalyst to avoid picking the wrong stick in a picking pin so the whole pile falls apart. There are great opportunities for business leaders to find which variables contribute to growth and which resources will later be unique. When resistance and bottlenecks form, it is about seeing the problems as opportunities and not falling too deep, but being able to correct speed, direction, and deliveries.

The ATLAS, including 150 insights

This is the working document that expands from the GUIDE to show how to solve the various concerns, issues, and bottlenecks that get in the way to your company's growth and success. In the upcoming chapters, five insights

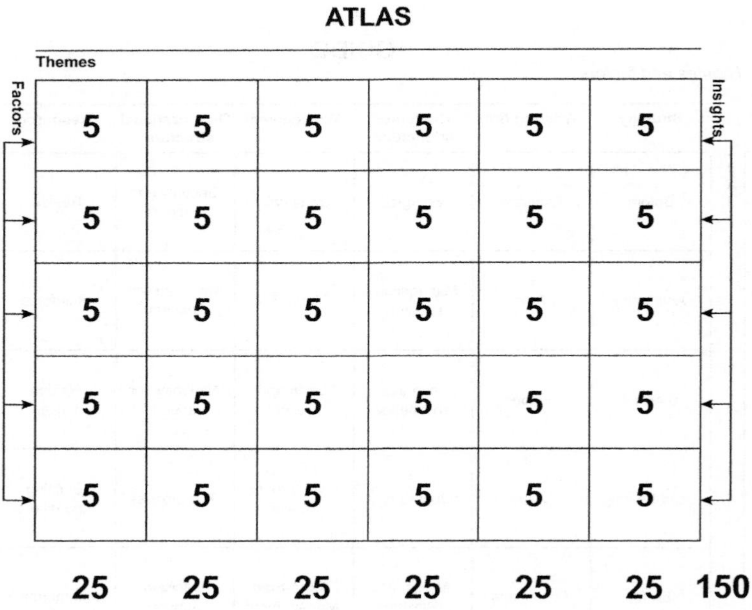

Figure 1.2 A perspective of the ATLAS containing five insights per factor leading to 150 insights.

at a time are presented within each of the success factors. These can act as directions for a project covering business model innovation and strengthen the development of a process and implementation.

At first glance, it is easy to see the themes, success factors, and insights as a wall of information that must be applied in order to see a successful outcome as a result of a change process, which is daunting. However, through asking questions, using these insights as keys to take apart a current company model, to understand which parts of the concept will unlock your journey, to take a closer look at how a business functions from order through to delivery and understand what works and what can be improved, it is possible to find pathways to build on existing systems and find exciting new possibilities. Using the images, a framework and structure are provided to refine questions and create a plan for growth that is based on the realities of the business at hand, generates predictable trajectories, and allows for more flexibility to continue evolving going into the future.[2]

Business model in perspective

Trade between countries has been going on for thousands of years, starting with the Silk Road between China and Rome. It then continued with luxury products from Arabia and the Muslim countries with spices on Sea Road until the 1500s, when Europe, and especially Great Britain, participated in the first Industrial Revolution. In the 1800s, great progress was made in astronomy, physics, mechanics, and shipping, and several countries also increased their land ownership in other parts of the world, particularly Spain, Holland, Portugal, along with others. The British led the way and global trade increased to almost 15 percent until World War I.

After that, trade increased in two different periods, from World War II to 1989 when the Iron Curtain to Eastern Europe fell that was created after the War. Later, the World Trade Organization (WTO) urged all countries to enter into free agreements and many countries did, and in 2001, China also joined. At the same time, the Internet had been created and suddenly orders could be placed all over the world and the opportunities increased. This provided opportunities to create global business models with different parts of a value chain produced in several locations around the world. Global trade soon reached a quarter of gross domestic product (GDP) and soon the sum of exports and imports exceeded 50 percent of world GDP, in some countries almost more than 100 percent, specifically in Singapore and Belgium. Now China and the United States dominate the fourth globalization focused on cyberspace, and there are also question marks around some negative effects around climate change.[3]

Since the early 1900s, there has been continuing technological development in transport and in information dissemination throughout the century. Information and its practical application has led to innovations that have totally reshaped our modern world, from communication to sending humans to the moon and allowing for exploration of deeper space through purpose-built technology. It has also led to a focus on transport, global travel, working in other countries, and cultural issues. Of course, the interest in foreign trade, exports and imports, and new opportunities has also helped shape the technological possibilities. In this development, a greater need for business models to understand and focus on customer needs has evolved.

Banks and multinational corporations are key players in the global world where it has become easier to produce remotely, international laws have been formed, languages have been adapted, and communication between people has been increased through renewed technology.[4] New opportunities have been created for the companies to find other customer areas and new revenue streams. It is nations, international companies, and people who together have created increased conditions for a larger market. The change has contributed to longer range for aircraft, more and faster railways, larger ships, increased container traffic on the oceans, and many new flexible innovations.[5]

Today, people can inform themselves through new technological methods developed with good business standards. The Internet and telephone have given us other opportunities to talk and communicate with each other. Social media is another evolution of people being able to express their opinions, choices, and beliefs.

A business model starts with seeking a customer with a certain need, a unique need. It's about finding strategies for customer needs within segments and choosing in which areas and then positioning the company

Business model

Segment	Customer	Relations	Channels	Value	Activities/ resources	Organization	Revenues
						Partners	Costs

Who/What	Why	Interact	Campaigns	Clarify buy	Unique set tangible and intangible	Structure/ choice	Value pay margin

Figure 1.3 A perspective on the entire value chain with choice of customers, key resources, structure, organization, and deliveries.[6]

toward that direction. The entire chain is built by understanding what the customer wants, developing relationships, choosing channels to reach out, and having an idea of customer value. From there, the business must be able to produce based on customer value with the right skills, in a structure and organization that can deliver finished services and products. Through close customer relationships, the concept can continue to develop value and increase the opportunities for safer growth with better margins. It is an independent situation between all parts that make up the chain and can be described with content, structure, and identifying who is within the chain.[7]

Strategy is a key tool for strengthening the company's competence by understanding the unique values ahead of its competitors.[8] When the chain of events is changed by replacing some actor or partner, then the model's conditions usually change for the better or worse. It can be about changing forward or backward in the chain, structuring the solution differently than before (usually shortening the chain) or among the parties involved by replacing or adding someone.[9]

Business model innovation

Global trade was helped after World War II in 1945 by the Bretton Woods system, which was a fixed-rate system for international currencies against the dollar. It regulated the exchange rates of member countries of the International Monetary Fund and its purpose was to simplify trade between countries from 1945 to 1971.[10] The system also led to the International Monetary Fund, the World Bank, and strengthened the United States as a superpower at the time.[11] Free flow of trade and capital has been an important piece of the puzzle for increased trade as well as a factor that has helped to improve the general standard of living.

Business model innovation

Anchoring	Force	Management	Opportunities	Margins/ costs	Reduce risks	Create process	Use knowledge
	Internal						
	External					Create time	Create project

Future beliefs	The reasons	Lead and steer	Mindset	Competitive profit	Everywhere	Show/ understand	Inventory/ early meeting

Figure 1.4 A perspective on different questions leading to a business model innovation project.

Today, many of the larger companies have their structure, organization, and partners scattered in several countries, which requires a management system that can lead and control, focus on the value of the entire business model, oversee control of margins, utilize careful planning, have well-thought-out communication, maintain developed relationships, and ensure good deliveries. As interest in how business models can be changed to meet increased competitiveness, the need to develop the existing model has also escalated in recent years. However, there are still few empirical studies that examine the business models and the factors that build success in a process of lasting profitable change.[12] The increased contact area not only enables more business but also increases the risk of misunderstandings and shortcomings in the business chain that can lead to bottlenecks.

A business model innovation process is about unlocking underlying values, trimming processes, and finding other solutions to the customer process. It is usually a creative process that takes time and effort. The reason behind why a process differs can be internal, external, or sometimes both. In order to get the best outcome and simplify later implementation, it is central to create consensus and clarify how the different resources should interact or what is actually missing.

My experience is that good business model innovation projects have a number of different variables that are important.

(1) Identify the purpose
(2) Understand the driving force behind the need (internally or/and externally)
(3) Review the existing business model/improve bottlenecks
(4) Conduct a review of resources
(5) Ensure anchoring with owners, boards and executive management
(6) Management team who can control and lead through others
(7) Set up a Three-Step Management structure
(8) Make sure there is a reasonable timetable
(9) Focus on opportunities
(10) Focus on improved margins or lover costs
(11) Go deeper in analyzing (reduce risks and identify bottlenecks)
(12) Understand the structure perplexity to control for speed
(13) Hold brainstorming seminars to identify the project
(14) Use the factors to select for a chart for implementation
(15) Prepare and develop a plan for implementation
(16) Make decisions on implementation including knowledge seminars
(17) Implement using the ATLAS
(18) Set out a reasonable schedule, management and have ambassadors

Figure 1.5 A perspective of important steps and variables in successful business model innovation.

The advent of creating new knowledge through innovations

Over the years, I have gradually developed a process and along the way secured the data, refined interview techniques, developed interview guides, and methodized how I have analyzed the projects. In most of the projects, I worked as an interviewer and later supported the implementation with troubleshooting seminars from the studies, laying the foundation for a possible implementation, knowledge seminars within the implementation, and mentoring with one-to-one meetings throughout the change.

One of the most recent intervention cases lasted almost three years and contained all the parts that a business model innovation case should have. It was about rapid growth, external impact, need for model development, great opportunities, production in several countries, a company that could develop with a good leader, there was a certain risk mindset, and a customer who wanted to grow further. The extensive intervention clearly showed that our themes and factors that were developed over a long period of time had merit as they helped the company on their successful journey.

The company grew by 150 percent, and profits went from 10 percent per year to close to 30 percent in year three. We identified about 30 projects from the early conclusions, made several alterations, and later built in a better backbone in the entire organizational solution. An important success factor was to locate the customer's unique value and improve the positions and solve for the entire business model in more countries. The average project is between two to three years in order to observe a complete innovation project and equal for mentoring. For sub-studies, it can be significantly shorter.

Expectations to be met by creativity

There are always high expectations for projects related to business model innovation. This applies regardless of the reasons why a process is needed but expectations can also be different between owner, board, and CEO. Most innovation projects are time-consuming and therefore I have seen the advantages of starting with mapping questions in early meetings and then correcting what can be corrected directly in the existing business model. This saves time and costs, which contribute to the gradual growth of consensus.

The expectations can also be different depending on the level at which the project is managed – from the board, management, or in a branch of business. Transparency and the opportunity to influence the outcomes are always central matters when the projects are planned and later implemented. There is often a fear on the part of owners and management to make problems visible and seek answers to which bottlenecks contribute negatively. Most often, the opportunities come as a more active part later, although it naturally differs from project to project and perhaps from which driving forces are involved.

The internal driving forces can be about changing business units, mergers or transfers in the organization, lack of certain internal competencies, changed leadership roles, and internal reports that are out of order. It may also be more directly due to the fact that collaborations do not work; the decision structure does not work; planning is lacking; information is too slow; demand looks different, which means that the tools no longer work; key employees are about to retire; management works differently in different companies or regions; there are problems between sales and production; different views on which segments should be leading; the distribution works worse due to a new player; and many more. The external forces are usually more related to market changes and are often about new or changing customer needs. The external questions are extremely important for larger companies because they are often quick and have a very big impact.

Selected cases, industries, and possibilities

In this book, I have chosen to work from my experience as an action researcher, with a focus on 28 customers, including 52 companies, and all data are anonymized. It is the framework with the themes, success factors, and insights that is interesting to you as a reader, and at the end I offer a deeper understanding of the book's concepts that you and your organization can use. I chose cases from the beginning in 1996 to the present day and about the same number from every six years. Of those selected customers, 50 percent of companies are global international organizations, 25 percent are national organizations in the European market, and 25 percent are local companies mainly from Scandinavia. All the selected companies are midsize or large companies with different types of owner structures.

In total, my chosen group has included 148 initial business meetings, 898 interviews, 532 unique seminars, 15 surveys, 38 focus groups, and 296 one-to-one meetings. It has been important to choose companies that have had a clear focus on solving problems, been working on several items at the same time, been affected by several driving forces, had mixed strategies, focused on their business models, used and developed their structures and organizations, and had several levels of management that have also been affected and been active in questioning their resources. They represent the fields of high technology, consumer goods, transport, general industry, service, resource, and consultants.

In the European Union's 27 member state countries, there are approximately 23 million companies, of which about 300,000 companies employ more than 50 people.[13] These companies still control close to about 40 percent of the workforce and a lot of the profits. If we use the same idea of above that about 1.5 percent of all companies in the world the potential use of the concepts in this book is extensive. Of course, even growing smaller companies can use the analysis methods and the attached aids at the end in parts or as objectives. However, the use is centered on larger companies that focus on constant development and want to use business model innovation as a basis for succeeding in a good and more secure transition. It's about working more broadly with resources and seeking answers in different ways.

Work on the book has intensified and has been tested against a number of the companies involved in the construction of the concepts. I have also taken in the views of leading experts, several industrialists and have conducted a number of seminars in the production of the book. They have also had the opportunity to influence the final product that you now hold in your hands.

Notes

1 Cecia Consulting AB, https://www.cecia.se.
2 So-rummet, "Science and Technology 1914–1991," https://www.so-rummet.se/kategorier/historia/det-korta-1900-talet/vetenskap-teknik-och-kommunikationer-1914-1991.
3 Peter Vanham, "A Brief History of Globalization," Geo Economics, World Economic Forum, January 17, 2019, https://www.weforum.org/agenda/2019/01/how-globalization-4-0-fits-into-the-history-of-globalization/.
4 M. Wolf, "Shaping Globalization," Finance & Development 51, no. 3 (2014): 22–25.
5 Klas-Göran Karlsson, Europe and the World in the 1900's (Stockholm: Liber AB, 2003).
6 Developed from Alex Osterwalder Business Model Canvas.
7 R. Amit and C. Zott, "Creating Value Through Business Model Innovation." MIT Sloan Management Review 53 (2012): 41–49.
8 D. J. Teece, "Business Models, Business Strategy and Innovation," Long Range Planning 43, no. 2–3 (2010): 172–94.
9 Amit and Zott, "Creating Value Through Business Model Innovation," 41–49.
10 Tom Petersson, History of Swedish Business 1864–2014, del IV: 1965–1985 (Stockholm: Dialogos Förlag, 2014).
11 So-rummet, "Science and Technology 1914–1991."
12 N. J. Foss and T. Saebi, "Fifteen Years of Research on Business Model Innovation: How Far Have We Come, and Where Should We Go?" Journal of Management 43, no. 1 (2016): 200–27.
13 Calculated from European Microfinance Network, https://www.european-microfinance.org/.

Chapter 2

Strategy

The first theme to consider when embarking on a business innovation project is strategy. This critical, but often overlooked, part of a business model can both set out the path forward through a change process while also taking care of some straightforward trimming of what is already working in a company to make strong gains. Strategy is overall about making plans in partnership with observations that allow for flexibility and evolution through a change process.

Improve before new growth

Globalization has continued since World War II, with improved transport opportunities, increased travel between countries, and continued technological development.[1] New opportunities have meant that companies have been able to expand their goods and services to more markets. An aircraft today can transport goods and people all over the world, something that used to be mostly for birds. The various airlines compete to transport safely, with good quality, provide reasonable prices, keep to schedules, and offer more sustainable alternatives. In line with increased demand, the world's ships have also become as large as the largest whales around the world's oceans, which can offer container traffic that facilitates and allows us to get goods from different places in the world.

The increased trade has been simplified by a freer supply of capital and trade, which has also made questions of import and export conditions central.[2] For a medium or large company that builds its business model in a larger market, the opportunities also increase the need to be able to adapt its deliveries. It may be that the company identifies the unique abilities in a particular country and decides to divide production in several countries. It may be that the cultural difference is beneficial from the point of view of productivity and cost. When companies operate in several markets, they have greater opportunities to find alternative resources and make adjustments that the environment requires. In a larger business solution, there are more

DOI: 10.4324/9781003402121-2

questions that a strategy can change along the way as distances increase, conditions between countries and regions differ, and several actors and parties are involved. It may seem obvious to make strategic improvements before a growth journey really takes off, but it is not always so.

Quite often, businesses start by looking at the human capital within their organization and may make changes to key positions in management. As companies change managers, there can sometimes be a vacuum for a strategy and it just rolls on until someone discovers that there has been a loss of market share. There may also be situations between business areas where things are going better than planned for an area and negatively affect the overall strategies. It's about carving out the best strategies to understand the industry and that the company can position itself with how they can create unique value for their customers.

The international company had a good reputation and had been around for a long time in several markets in the Nordic region. They were market leaders but feared that competition would increase as more international players were about to establish themselves.

The strategies from the existing customer group needed to be expanded into a comprehensive project organization with more active planning, collaboration, documentation, time, and finances. There were questions about the dilemma around products and pricing and how future total sales would be affected in the new segment. A change in strategy would affect the business model and they understood that larger industrial deliveries would certainly force the company to get even closer to its customers and, above all, focus in a different way. They decided to conduct an initial customer study to map existing strategies and build a new basis for decision-making.

After studies and a number of developing seminars, it emerged that the target groups were different and they lacked a management solution to scale-up more of the projects that had a completely different process and less sales. They decided to improve, simplify, and communicate the existing model better with a focus on margins and deliveries. They decided to wait with a project organization for a new segment and gather more data ahead for a later decision.

For business innovation projects, it is important to understand what role strategy has played in the company in the past and how they want it to work going into the future. We see major differences between leaders and how some companies want a fairly loose structure that can be adapted where others instead want clear support to be able to move forward. A strategy can be strategic, tactical, or operational in these environments. What we advocate is that it be clear if and how it should govern a changed business model. It is important to understand what role strategy plays in the potential for improvement.

We have also encountered situations several times when the strategies have been ready for the parent company, but it does not reach one of the subsidiaries because their manager still works according to the old model. It can be difficult to change strategies when they have been around for a long time because people have learned behaviors according to the knowledge needed to be able to deliver the best customer experience. When it then turns out that the best customer experience is no longer the one that the subsidiary delivers as part of a larger whole, it may be made clear in early bottlenecks or that internal dissatisfaction begins to develop among the sister companies or in the main company itself. A conflict has developed between doing a task according to a past behavior and doing it the right way.

> The subsidiary in the large group had had the same CEO for the past 20 years, who had started in the company as a project manager. In the past two years, the business had pivoted from major project deliveries to delivering simple services to the parent company, which had also appointed a new CEO.
>
> When we got the assignment, two consulting groups had already had to leave the project because the previous behavior was protected by an informal group inside the company going up against the old CEO and almost no one at the company wanted to work with the parent company's simpler solutions.
>
> We created a change project that started by understanding the differences in strategies between parent and subsidiary companies. The conflict was clear not only between the employees but had also spread to the customers. Therefore, we started with a mapping of the strategies backwards, including deliveries and assignments between the companies.

It can often be enough to set the strategies better instead of offering more strategies. This works to clarify the choices on which the previous strategies were based and is useful if introducing new strategies would compete with being unique. There are big gains in taking stock of the existing strategies before an innovation case takes off. As companies become more numerous, there is a risk that the messages are diluted and not perceived in the same way and the different leadership functions may not communicate consistently to all those concerned.

Since a change project often benefits from strategies to support implementation, these need to serve as a foundation in building the new corrected business model with other behaviors. As with building a new home on existing foundations, there are advantages to knowing whether it is a masonry foundation, for example, or a plinth foundation, basement foundation or crawl space in order to proceed with continuing to plan for what is to come. The strategies set the direction forward and become the security for the project while the business continues. When an inventory of them is already being carried out, it is beneficial to also focus on what can be done in a better, simplified way.

> We got a call from an existing international customer about a major project at a current international supplier and they wondered if we were interested. They told us that the company had operations in several countries and the head office was in Europe. The company had bought several businesses and needed to make improvements to its business model.
>
> The company had a turnover of SEK 400 million and the project was about saving SEK 20 million by making alternative revenues visible and putting pressure on processes and everyone in the supply chain. We conducted our business meetings and when we were about to start the collaboration to map out the possibilities two weeks later we needed to stop.
>
> We discovered that the CEO had already started several good projects after two meetings so he wanted to remove these good projects and search further with others. Then he also wanted to reduce the conversations and for us to deliver our views after each of the planned 20 interviews. Despite the scope of the contract, we chose to decline. We saw that the business innovation project did not have a clear purpose, did not have a management team, and would not be able to cope with having the planned project at the same time.

When inventory is done, we usually also carry out a review of improvements for all strategies. The review makes it possible to clarify what the different strategies are used for, what they mean, and if there is anything that contributes to measuring. Close to 100 percent of our customers have set existing strategies in the business when we start. Some are very blurry while others incredibly clear and business-governing. It's different every time and gives an interesting insight into the workings of the company before work begins on refining or introducing new strategies.

It is interesting to find that over the past five years, more and more strategies have become more personal in tone. They have touched on the personal aspects of work/life balance while blurring certain boundaries between work, home, and leisure. COVID-19 has contributed to even more momentum in that change. The question, however, is what happens moving forward with these shifting boundaries? In any case, conducting a review is something that we recommend before any new changes or strategies are introduced.

Insights for improving strategy before new growth

1. Clarify role for implementation
2. Understand behaviors from existing business model (resistance)
3. Conduct an inventory of the existing strategies
4. Understand the personal concerns (work, home, and leisure)
5. Improve with review and trimming

Ensure anchoring for new strategies and clarify what can strengthen anchoring

In the larger world market, goods and services are moving faster than before and companies have gradually adapted their units accordingly.[3] International issues deal with more perspectives and it soon goes as fast as on a high-speed train. The cultural, political, and social perspectives are mixed with questions about the best financial conditions, best economic solutions, and increasingly, a focus on the ecological ones. When companies' business solutions contain more parameters, actors, and partners to create customer value, it also places higher demands on consensus for all parties, in the same way as there are expectations on behavior and destination for all passengers in a bus.

The owners of multinational companies need to understand more market conditions, boards need to be more active in their roles, and group CEOs should spend a lot of time anchoring via data. We notice that today's leaders of large companies are more interested in data while also relying on intuition, so they have fewer backup staff and make smarter choices based on accumulated information.[4] It is more crucial today to anchor the strategies carefully and ensure that everyone involved understands the meaning of the business model. The cultural aspect is an important part where views on work and remuneration may differ. The new strategies need an anchoring that is clear to the different groups and that remains the same regardless of whether it is about the entire company, parts of the company, or product areas. This can of course be influenced by the form of the group, for example, where family companies perhaps prefer more informal decision-making paths more than others and prepare decisions for a little while longer for fewer hands.

It is an easy enough thing to look at strategies in a company, see where changes can be made, then take off in that direction without taking the time to understand where these changes are coming from. The desire to make snap decisions based on working with something that is familiar (such as a strategy that has been in place for a long time) when seeing that a tweak may be all that is necessary may be strong but must be tempered. In proceeding forward without considering the implications of a strategic shift and anchoring that change by clarifying what is going to happen with all parts of the production chain, there is a risk that action is taken prematurely or without having the chance to assess the conditions within the business.

A change often requires a redistribution of the existing conditions, and in a growing business model, this may mean that more people are added. Efficiency is part of how these people and processes interact in a solution but also how they are structured and that the resources are actually available when they are needed. These are usually very sensitive and complex issues when resources are to be given space for strategic conversations. We see it again and again that strategies help companies move forward but that the obstacles are also there, particularly misconceptions in communication, cultural differences, and sometimes laws. Most people would not get on a bus without knowing what the trip costs, how long the trip takes, what seats and legroom look like, and above all ensuring that the trip goes where we want to travel.

They were an international manufacturer that operated in several different markets and were number two to three in most product groups in Sweden. The company had made several acquisitions in the past four years and now the direction needed to be clearer. A major market survey in Denmark showed that the Nordic needs would increase and there was room for more specialized products in their niche.

The various acquisitions had worked well and deliveries had improved significantly over the past year from their factories. The Nordic office decided to conduct an extensive external and customer study to strengthen its decision-making basis for a possible future change in strategies. The study included retailers and the key end customers who could be identified.

After the initial pilot study, additional interesting people/companies were added to the qualitative customer study. The company chose to strengthen its positions by developing new strategies for a completely unique product group and at the same time to reduce some cheaper alternatives that it had offered previously. The new strategies would provide additional opportunities to grow to number one in the market, management reasoned.

When we work with innovations in companies, we try to understand what kind of timescale can work for the project. This means knowing what space the project needs for understanding and how that need for understanding will meet the overall needs. Of course, it is impossible to answer in initial conversations, but as the qualitative interviews begin to be conducted, it is perhaps too late to get these questions on the table. There needs to be room for increased understanding, whether it is adjusted strategies due to bottlenecks or completely new strategies to be prioritized.

A major challenge for the business innovation model case is the expectation that the owner, board, or management must handle. Coming in at the beginning there can sometimes be the thought that it is enough to simply identify the need for change and then work to find where those alterations can be made in the shortest time possible. We have noticed over time that there are time savings in creating time for renewal right from the start. The calm managers do more to trim the strategies before starting the resource changes. It is possible to start collecting resources without switching too much into the strategies and if things go too fast, the company can end up at dead ends and start again and again. The focused leader usually starts by refining the already-existing strategies.

> *The international group of companies had operations in more than seven countries and was the market leader in its segment of its industry. When COVID-19 shut down operations, it had immediate effects on the company, which from one day to the next lacked revenue for its many operations.*
>
> *This dramatic event caused the owners, board, and management to act even more together than before. In the end, more capital was needed, changes were made in delivery capacity with redundancy and notice and, in the short term, a different business model. It transitioned from data governance to general considerations, but the course did not change although survival strategies were prioritized immediately.*
>
> *Three years later, management notes that the quick decisions to collaborate, focus, and believe in the existing model also contributed to many employees later being able to be rehired.*

We have seen that when companies focus and strengthen their existing processes, it automatically creates understanding. This is because most of the people involved in the company are familiar with the processes from their everyday work, so it is more a case of comprehending a slight shift rather than having to integrate new information. It is usually less challenging for the company to make corrections before a major innovation project. It can both help clarify already-existing strategies and lay the foundation for the upcoming project. Evaluating and planning strategies in an upcoming project is a factor for success going into the future. It saves time, encourages greater understanding, and usually generates a willingness to contribute to doing something better.

There are times when in clarifying a strategy it is discovered that larger-scale changes to the existing model are needed. The major dramatic changes affecting entire communities often add an additionally difficult dimension to the planning of projects. It may be about resource changes in raw materials that create shortages, redundancies of their own employees, partners that need to be replaced, or completely changed needs of consumers. These external changes affect industries and companies and can change businesses very quickly. Strategies tend to work best when they are direct, focused, and prioritized. Without this organization of thinking, there are many more assumptions in these rapid changes that can slow the effectiveness of changes in strategy. The really big changes need other types of strategies and should not be part of an innovation project.

A larger medium-sized group of companies had oriented their previous local strategies toward national and international solutions over many years. These were larger contracts for service and consulting. The development had gone very well and now the business was no longer in line with the strategies.

The dominant customer wanted to buy central agreements, have more advisory input, and simplify administration. The company would implement a change called for by the largest customer from 12 locations to a regional solution. The company chose to follow its large customer and 12 operations became three regions and all former managers had to apply for the advisory jobs and the regional manager roles.

It was a difficult change that also created internal frustrations as it meant a completely new business model with changed leadership, changed services, and the dismissal of several local partners in favor of national procurements. The company hired an external CEO with previous change experience to manage the new management team and the upcoming situation. We conducted a qualitative study and one-to-one meetings, together with six seminars, to solve many of the upcoming questions along the way.

In the past making assessments in clarifying strategies relied heavily on being able to lean on the team working in a company to get the information that was needed to get a complete understanding. Before computerization in the 1990s, the top manager often hired more staff to support their decisions. Today, many of these roles can be handled via communication from systems. What is probably most challenging today is that most people are more informed than ever before. A CEO who is going to change their entire company might prefer to bring in external help to substantiate their factual decisions and prepare arguments for their strategies. Extra support is needed for the person ultimately responsible for the project either through the board, the CEO (if it is a subsidiary) or through external support.

It has become more challenging to be a CEO today because of fast changes in the environment, the communication tools available, and the overall possibilities to revise facts. We see a change in large companies where CEOs also have more outgoing commitments and questions are handed on to fewer people than before. They must better strengthen their brands, be forward thinking and at the same time have time to control and be responsible for their companies. Listed companies also demand their responsibility with clear, well-thought-out, and delivering strategies. A new CEO today can more actively seek information about the stories that built the company they are going to be working with, but the CEO may still only hear the positive feedback and not the difficult negative criticism. Therefore, these people need to not only have an outgoing personality with social skills but also be human, caring, and listening. The CEO or manager needs to have qualities that support the company's existing strategies.

Insights for anchoring strategies and clarifying the anchoring

1. Create space for understanding
2. Refine, evaluate, and plan future strategies
3. Major changes require other strategies
4. Support from decision-makers
5. Managers need to have self-control qualities

Simplify implementation

In the 1800s, we experienced an agricultural revolution where goods were mainly transported by horse and carriage, boats, and in the latter half of the century, by train. From the early 1900s and throughout the next almost 100 years, technology changed our conditions dramatically in transport and communication but also in other areas. Industrial development began to grow and conditions were created for transporting by airplanes, helicopters, cars, and trucks.[5]

The great opportunities in a more open market have driven technological development, and through freer access to capital, new innovations have also been created to communicate more. The information has evolved from turntables, telephones, radio, TV, large computers, smaller computers, mobile phones, iPad, and the Internet.[6] From becoming settled in the 1800s, we can now communicate directly with each other throughout almost the entire world. The security of all systems that move communications and data is the next frontier in technology to ensure that information remains secure. The world has become more accessible but also smaller. We have become closer together and the national borders have been blurred and are created again and again.

Technological development was driven to a large extent by the great wars of the 1900s, particularly World War I and World War II. There was a race between different nations and states for technological development, which contributed to it going faster and faster. The increased globalization with the growth of multinationals from the 1950s has also increased the importance and need to communicate between people in the companies and as more and more people began to travel and work internationally. The development also meant more uniform conditions between countries, and several Western countries created public institutions for better living standards.

The technological development of recent decades has enabled faster communication, and at the same time it has increased the demands for clarity. When things move quickly, there are also risks that we do not perceive the message or simply misunderstand. The technological development of communicating quickly via e-mail, mobiles, and other platforms allows us to receive a message but not necessarily attend it; we move so quickly that we don't take time to understand the message we've received, so it's possible that we take action based on a cursory reading rather than consideration of what is being asked of us. The news is on TV and available via the Internet so the old paper newspapers are looking for other business models to survive. The younger generations have a technological user advantage and large groups of parents do not know what their children are doing online.

This speed and access to information translates into the working world often with mixed results. Those who have been in the workforce for a longer period of time have to take on not only their roles in the workplace but often additional learning to be able to use and manage hardware and systems that are brought in as technology improves. Younger workers can bring in existing knowledge of the hardware of the workplace and ideas of how to streamline systems, particularly if they are early adopters of new tech.[7] However, in working at this faster pace they may put less time into communication by using abbreviations that others are unfamiliar with or may be put off reading lengthy e-mails from their colleagues. This leads to the possibility of friction between coworkers with misunderstandings or the perception that one group doesn't take the work seriously or that the other can't possibly understand because they aren't as up to date on the systems within the company.

A larger partner-owned company faced a management buyout where the existing owners would retire and management would buy their own and others' shares. The company used to have many stories of successful ownership changes but now the items were bigger because the value growth had been fantastic for much of their ownership.

The younger employees had difficulty understanding some of the older people's rather long and detailed strategies. The new management was judged to lack the necessary experience and expertise, which is why a new CEO had been recruited and offered the opportunity to participate in the buyout.

To reinforce the upcoming implementation, the company decided to spend more time on clarification and invited customers to participate. After a qualitative owner study together with customers, a strategy began to be chiseled out in several management seminars. The new strategies were aimed at new industries and with a positioning focused on quality and sustainability.

We have noticed that the best processes have anchored strategies that affect the direction, but that it is also important to have an understanding that can be angled from several directions. It works better when the strategies are short and clear and have an explanation that is understandable to many. At our seminars, we train the business model and break it down into smaller components, which enables shorter and clearer strategies. It is the same as the way sports teams say "we're going to find a way to win" to strengthen themselves when they feel inferior before the big game. In innovation projects, it is about short, clear, and logical strategies. It is always for the company to understand the industry positioning and think twice to find its unique customer value.

Strategies that are not direct, focused, and lack an order of priority often run into problems. Many times, it is the projects that do not get power to the direction of travel, in the same way that a car runs out of gasoline or electricity in the wilderness; then it takes a lot to replenish or charge. The strategies need to be easy to communicate to motivate and ensure the direction of travel.

A relatively newly established company with about 100 employees had, in a short time, secured several new contracts that involved the operation and development of care. The new situation was challenging for several businesses where new areas and clear structures were needed to lead through others.

The contracts contained far-reaching responsibilities for behavior. At the same time, the company wanted to contribute toward authorization to be able to hire fewer people. Their own conclusions were that clarifying the strategies could help the overall business solution find its developed form in the different deliveries as there were different business units.

We conducted qualitative studies and participated in focus groups with companies and customers. The old strategies were refined and communicated clearly to the selected segments to add more customers but in other industries.

In business model innovation projects, it is important that the strategies have a good beginning and a clear end. When we conduct improvement seminars after completed studies, we talk about technology even around our meetings, marking out a defined beginning and a strongly established conclusion. For strategies, it can be about the next strategy taking over in a chain of choices and as such defining the parameters is essential. The start is linked to our focus on the place that we want the groups to use in their creation of strategies. It is an important piece of the puzzle to build in a gradual evaluation and slowly improve the focus over time. The strategies need to have a good beginning and clear endings.

A larger service company had had setbacks in lost business, management affected by private events, and some ownership questions that overshadowed the trust of the business. There had been clear, well-structured, and forward-looking strategies, but the setbacks had meant that the strategies died out and disappeared along the way.

The group decided to draw strength from the existing customers with a qualitative study. They invited employees, suppliers, and customers into their study. In total, the change was the start of a new journey to respond differently and search for new strategies.

It led to new trimmed strategies and a change of CEO within the ownership group, clearly higher goals, and help from some of the larger customers to secure deliveries from potential new customers in other areas.

It does not always have to be numbers to be measured when an overall vision can be explained by turnover, share of market, or number of employees. In business models that do not work, the focus on direction is something that contributes to incipient bottlenecks between partners who do not have resources or if there are few responsible employees, ones who do not deliver on the amount of effort that is part of the business solution and choose to finish the work before it is completed. This type of conflict is very time-consuming, and it is usually because the strategies are weak, management is lacking, and communication has disappeared. The better companies who are able to adapt use the steering instruments as leverage for the trades to be carried out as planned the better. To simplify understanding, it can also facilitate that the strategies are accountable, measured, and completed.

It is also about whether the innovative work needs to get someone to rely on to ensure the investment and implementation. It is one of the most important success factors in simplifying the implementation of the projects to actually work with numbers, preferably a profit and loss accounts that reflect the project. There is so much that is difficult to measure when the projects are complex, but at the company level we have several good examples where the measurement has mainly been used for feedback for the employee's performance.

Insights for simplification of strategies to simplify implementation

1. Develop short, clear, and logical strategies
2. Possible to communicate to justify the change
3. Good beginning and clear ends
4. Understanding should be responsible, measurable, and completed
5. Work with number to justify the implementation (important)

Strategy should be load-bearing, leading, and communicative

The international market feels closer with today's communication, and as overall, the general standard of living has increased worldwide. We have been better off as life has become more flexible and innovations have increased. With the expansion of the international market, more countries have also begun to compete for patents dominated by China and the United States, but India is emerging in advanced data analytics, machine learning, and protective cybersecurity technologies. Applications for global patents have increased from 1 million in 1995 to over 3 million in 2021, but above all it is China and Asia that have constantly increased (Asia 67.6 percent) and the United States and Europe have decreased (North America 18.5 percent, Europe 10.5 percent) along with some smaller countries.[8] England also shadows the two dominant countries in advanced radio frequency communications, advanced optical communications, and artificial intelligence (AI) algorithms and hardware accelerators.

For business model innovation, it is, above all, signals and driving forces that trigger changes and affect the companies directly. We see not only new external issues that are increasing in line with air pollution, droughts, wildfires, plastic pollution, biodiversity loss, and sea level increases but also new emerging technologies such as AI and not least the Internet.[9] It's about finding standards for strategies that do standardized things. New areas create new opportunities but also many questions and above all more responsibility for those who own the issues. It's no longer possible to just sit down and wait for the answers; leaders have to move forward and seek the answers.

The strategies for the new tools need more to work and connect even more closely with values that the recipient can feel and understand. It is about how we as users also search for our information and how we communicate; therefore, more proximity to customer needs is required than before. It does not work with a longer product strategy when the product is already to be replaced after six months by some newer variant with sharper and better performance. The products that are not sold could previously be entered in a balance sheet, but what is not sold today usually has no value at all or negligible values. It's like running a marathon and running the wrong way a mile before the finish and missing it, thereby missing the result. Communication and its effects have never been more important.

Our experience shows that it does not always help to have good strategies for business models, but an innovation project can help and strengthen the relationships in the structure. The business has content and is organized according to a structured idea of how the product or service should be delivered and with which actors or partners. The strategies become stronger if it signals a value, a real value that can be based on targets that are responsible, measurable, and complete. The value-creating strategies also need to be understood and communicated to the point where everyone involved has the same idea of where they are going in their unique customer delivery.

The group management in a larger group had bought its company a few years ago with the idea of delivering unique solutions to families who were at the beginning of their family formation and wanted to live better.

Concept development focused on offering a good enough product at a reasonable price in areas where there were potential buyers. They had a combined experience from larger companies and were able to put together several components into one potential product. The partly new strategies relied on building houses for this new customer group and needed to be built with solid arguments.

After doing several studies on how much cost went to rent, how far an average family was prepared to move, interviews with already completed areas and actually analyzing all available secondary data, a concept was formed that focused on a group that was previously not able to get nice houses. This created value-laden, empathetic, and long-term strategies and with quick results because it was possible to communicate with all the necessary data behind the decisions.

When strategies become value-laden, it is often that at the same time they also have empathy, something that makes the need clear and is close to the customer. It is a softer value that we can help focus on when using development seminars in connection with implementation. Above all, it is about the model showing an understanding of the customer's perspective and distinguishing a feeling outside the model. This is the point at which they get the opportunity to be involved and have an influence.

The growing midsize consulting company was fantastic at valuing its various concepts, and in line with more and larger assignments, the need for an external overview together with customers increased.

The strategy questions were about whether there were additional services to offer, which services were most appreciated, and how the benefit could be assessed based on the total delivery. The company thought this could be the answer for scaling dramatically and offering a more unique delivery.

We conducted an extensive customer study and also met competitors. In total, we conducted about 15 seminars that included market knowledge, negotiation techniques, argumentation, and how the concepts could be further adapted. For the value part, a possible subscription was also created and provided completely new recurring revenue. When the company was later sold a few years later, the subscription was something that was involved in deciding the acquisition.

We spend a lot of time ensuring that management understands the importance of having leading strategies that are empathetic and can be analyzed before, during, and after an implementation. Follow-up is an important cornerstone for success and management needs to give its consent to these supportive, leading, and communicative strategies. Our experience from over thousands of seminars is that it can be difficult to get close to strategies that are used in large companies for planning, but gradually these are very appreciated elements. These are also issues that can remain close to management and help empower people in the organization who participate and implement the change projects.

The holding company included number of companies and had its energy items separated into its own subsidiary in order to be able to create more unique values for resources, set clear goals, and work with mapping within its internal processes. The company also worked with external customers to compare its internal cutting-edge expertise, which contributed very positively.

Despite the separated responsibilities, there was a clear idea of how the business model should be managed and where the strategies would more accurately contribute. The most important component was to ensure the value of different resources and clarify measurement effects on an ongoing basis.

There was a consensus between owners and management, which simplified continued work with refined strategies and improvements in the business format. Several interview studies were conducted together with seminars for management and then follow-up activities. It led to refined strategies and a new way of planning the business solution.

In working with the strategies' connection to the business model, there are great advantages in assessing the significance and trying to create a profit center that the more detailed strategies can work with together. For business model innovation cases, the measurement depends on where they are needed and what the project covers, either the entire business or a department. We have used target images for a long time and think that it often works very well, including in analyzing potential revenues, margins on purchases, and other costs. It is a prerequisite that the needs of the business model are mapped in order for the strategies to have effective access to solution.

Insights for creating the arguments that the strategies should be load-bearing and leading

1. Stronger if they signal a value
2. Stronger if they are empathic
3. Must be carrying, leading, and communicative
4. Target images works very well: vision
5. Effectiveness mapped against existing business model

Living strategies, close to the customer and successful development with follow up

As the international market demands new services and products, the larger companies also need to change their business models and pay closer attention and be more active than before. The next generation called Alpha, born in 2010 or later, by 2025, will be more than 2 billion worldwide. They are about to enter working life and they have grown up with access to new information and tools available today. How will they want their information moving forward and what will they want to communicate around? Will they want to settle in the countryside far from cities or do they want to live in cities? Maybe they will have to break the norm of work and housing.[10] Price developments may force them to live in collectives or because they want to communicate more in groups and rather find their own norms for a good life. The biggest challenge and risk are the climate change that generations before have created.

The mobility of money, labor, and travel also gives hope as the standard of living has increased. New technology will create other solutions in the fields of nano-technology, education, biotech, and information. Edge computing, machine learning, AI, and robotic processing are some areas that will create many other behaviors and probably even jobs. Interest in behavioral science and the rich data that comes with qualitative interviews has increased as companies have become more open, accessible, and diversified with operations in more markets. The older generation has learned to measure everything and economists have decided to focus on productivity, but what if the vast majority do not want to measure and instead want to feel and socialize?

Living strategies are a new feature that sees a use for linking strategies and behaviors better than ever before. Technological development has contributed to people having greater transparency and being influenced from many directions at the same time. Some projects have been prominent in highlighting how vital this linking is and shows where it has been clear that it has taken more time than in previous strategy models to create understanding and motivation. Most transition projects contain resistance in various forms from internal systems, people, or external partners. This enables companies to come more actively closer, now that work is actually a mix of going to work or being able to work with a computer from a café or from home.

> *The company had about 250 employees and had operated in more than 15 different cities around the country for a long time. It delivered services to a segment within a large industry. They were market-dominant and the company's owners reasoned that with technological developments there could be a future threat.*
>
> *The first project that we worked on looked at where the technological development really changed the business model at the start of the company. It was about completely changing the business and offering the service via a system instead of something that had previously been done manually.*
>
> *We conducted an annual study with over 100 interviews, long-term analyses, various seminars, and later also ongoing one to one with key employees. Our role was still research and acting as catalysts. It was a large and comprehensive study that was about converting a company from about 250 employees in many locations to about 40 people in a more centralized location when everything would be ready. Four years later, it was a reality with higher revenues and better results.*

There are times when it may seem that creating these living strategies becomes difficult, such as when a company is larger or has many subsidiaries or regions. However, it is often the case that this is when they are most needed and most effective. Living strategies should be used when the projects are larger, affect more people, and there is need for a deeper change that often takes longer. By engaging more people in bigger projects, it is often necessary that it take a longer period of time when the change is implemented. It is about creating attention, clarifying a living example, and helping to change the company based on the company's own culture. By doing so, this allows the strategies to take root in a way that is meaningful to everyone in the company as they will recognize it as an extension of their existing culture and way of doing business. This will mean that a new strategy will not just exist in the boardroom and manager offices. The deeper impact hits further down the organization and starts conversations between managers and employees. It is important that the issues are rooted and that the management structure supports the attention that these living examples can be. A good start is to map out the company's overall culture.

Living examples should primarily be directed toward choices that help the daily work, even if it is a business model innovation case where only certain identified projects will be introduced into the ongoing business. It can be about showing how Chris works at the lathe and his entire work routine. It can also be about showing Morgan's work as a quality manager and the resistance that she encounters when she books meetings, requests reports and compiles them for a variety of purposes. In most cases, these are positive images and good examples. The living strategies are used based on how the company understands the industry, does its positioning, and how the unique value is created.

> The international group operated in several countries and one of their subsidiaries had had delivery problems for a long time due to a shortage of certain materials and could not deliver completely. This led to an increase in tied-up capital while the customer continued to order more and more.
>
> The young management had the power of the growth of recent years and received ongoing knowledge replenishment through the tasks of cross function. This situation required something extra because the premises gradually became overcrowded with about unfinished and undelivered products.
>
> By creating a number of seminars with live strategies, we were able to quickly find alternative internal solutions and ensure that the company had to deliver from about 90 percent. It helped in the short term to create vivid examples to turn into a positive feeling for the company. It was about the groups coming together and creating new ones.

Live strategies should be part of the daily choices to primarily help the larger business model innovation cases. They should be prioritized so that the chain is tighter and more focused and enables the chain to go faster and ensures that it does not stop. It is an important part between the more traditional strategies and the existing business model.

When the projects are more extensive, they usually include a larger study with more interviews and it is there that some questions can be focused on processes and improvements. It is not the communications department that handles the management, but it is a designated change group that gets approval to build this communication into the management functions. In larger companies, there are often stories and myths about going back to the foundation of the organization. Therefore, living strategies are an accepted way of communicating as they utilize the same kind of storytelling and communication style. They should be treated as living stories that are retold. Competitions can also be created as an additional instrument to support the processes so that it becomes an interactive process.

> *The large group had been led by two different CEOs in the last five years, and by the last shift in management, they had divided their strategies into two groups, the world and Europe. Within these segments, there were also several divisions.*
>
> *To further strengthen the implementation, the company needed to change parts of its business solution and in some regions very radically. The ambition was to offer a full-service range in the long term and change the pricing.*
>
> *We started with one-to-one strategies and conducted a qualitative study in several countries. After that, the company worked on the implementation of corrected and clear strategies.*

Live strategies can be the difference between what the company wants to happen and what actually happens. In larger companies, more activity is required to be able to create a change. Strategies are tasked with supporting, leading, and helping to develop the value of the business model. These strategies can also be helpful between generations and, above all, in increasingly diversified companies. There is a major challenge in changing existing business models and today's society. We also see that living strategies can be what is needed to create power in environmental transitions and sustainability issues. It is, above all, previous behaviors that constitute the opposite in a change and there we see that a project organization does not really resemble anything else when we carry out the projects.

Insights for creating living strategies

1. Support larger projects in larger organizations
2. Should capture attention, highlight, and reinforce a company
3. Should describe daily activities
4. Should be tighter, more focused, and prioritized
5. Should be helpful between generations and diversified companies

Summary

Strategy is something that businesses of all sizes take time to create, but so often they choose to set it in stone rather than making it something dynamic that can be a driver of change. While having something strong in place at the beginning of a company's journey can set out the choices forward, without the capacity for change, over time it can be the very thing that creates roadblocks to growth and success. It is at the same time the most important thing a company can create to define itself as well as being the element that can present the biggest challenges. It is about understanding what value the company can create within the chosen industry and how they position themselves.

Before embarking on any meaningful change in a business model, it is key to look at opportunities to examine and improve existing strategies within an organization. There must be clarification of the role that strategy plays in implementation, understand if there are existing behaviors that make it difficult to do correctly, make an inventory of the existing strategies, and carry out an improvement in the existing strategies with review and trimming. By taking time at the outset to determine what already exists within the organization that can be reoriented toward improving processes, it clears the path for where new interventions can generate positive change.

As strategies are introduced, it is essential that these are anchored and clarified within the company at all levels holistically. From the beginning, space is needed for understanding the incoming project, existing strategies must be refined at the outset, and evaluation and plans for future strategies must take place. It is also important that major changes are identified and separate strategies are prepared for those changes. With new processes and actions taking place, extra support is required for the person who is leading the charge, which will help to ensure that they have the characteristics needed to be in line with the strategies that have been set out.

Whenever change is going to be brought into an organization, potential bottlenecks can be solved by simplifying the implementation of updated strategies. From the outset, short, clear, and logical strategies must be developed and they should be possible to communicate to justify the change. When strategies are logical, they have a good beginning and a clear, definable ending. Finally, to simplify understanding, the strategy should be responsible, measurable, and completed.

Strategies that are going to have a long-term effect and positive change cannot only be the paper they are written on or the minutes taken in the meeting; they have to be load-bearing and leading. Strategies will become stronger if they signal a value and if they are empathetic. As changes take place, follow-up becomes important in the carrying, leading, and communicative strategies. As part of strategy leading and being load-bearing effectively, it must be mapped against the business model. If a strategy can't lead or carry the load of change, it can fall apart and soon any upward trends in change may stall or stop all together.

There are many ways of developing strategies for change, but to ensure that they will be dynamic and reactive if they need to be, they need to be living as a part of the company and therefore able to adapt as circumstances alter across time. While some may argue that larger companies are too complex for something as radical as a living strategy, they are in fact very well suited for larger projects in larger organizations. When functioning well, they capture attention while highlighting and reinforcing a company. Again, rather than being something that is handled by management, living strategies go deeper and will hit further down the organization all the way to the shop floor. This is because they describe daily activities and are tighter, more focused, and prioritized in a way other strategies are not.

When compared to strategies that are more traditional or rigid, living strategies can be the difference between what the company wants to happen and what actually happens. These strategies can also be helpful between generations and, above all, increasingly diversified companies. Living strategies can be what is needed to create power in environmental transitions and sustainability issues. Overall, a living strategy is one that can be an engine that not only makes change achievable but is also able to radically alter outcomes in business model innovation.

In our modern and rapidly changing world, with all the amazing advances in technology constantly altering the face of business in all sectors, strategy may seem like an obvious driver of change. However, it is very often underutilized and aspects of it overlooked. By addressing strategy at the outset of change and taking the time to evaluate existing structures before introducing new strategic changes, it provides an opportunity to access growth that can be carried forward through all aspects of business model innovation.

Notes

1 Peter Vanham, "A Brief History of Globalization," Geo Economics, World Economic Forum, January 17, 2019, https://www.weforum.org/agenda/2019/01/how-globalization-4-0-fits-into-the-history-of-globalization/.
2 So-rummet, "Science and Technology 1914–1991," https://www.so-rummet.se/kategorier/historia/det-korta-1900-talet/vetenskap-teknik-och-kommunikationer-1914-1991.
3 Vanham, "A Brief History of Globalization."
4 Marcy Farrell, "Data and Intuition: Good Decisions Need Both," Harvard Business Publishing Corporate Learning, January 6, 2023, https://www.harvardbusiness.org/data-and-intuition-good-decisions-need-both/.
5 Vanham, "A Brief History of Globalization."
6 Kevin Webb, "From the Internet to the iPhone, Here Are the 20 Most Important Inventions of the Last 30 Years," Insider, May 17, 2019, https://www.businessinsider.com/most-important-inventions-of-last-30-years-internet-iphone-netflix-facebook-google-2019-5?op=1&r=US&IR=T.
7 Jennifer Jordan and Michael Sorell, "Why Reverse Mentoring Works and How to Do It Right," Harvard Business Review, October 3, 2019, https://hbr.org/2019/10/why-reverse-mentoring-works-and-how-to-do-it-right.
8 Johnny Wood, "The Number of Global Patent Applications Is Breaking Records: Where Are the Hotspots?" Forum Agenda, World Economic Forum, December 19,

2022,   https://www.weforum.org/agenda/2022/12/innovation-patent-filings-intellectual-property-ip-applications/.

9   Meetings Coverage, "As Humanity's Environment Footprint Becomes Increasingly Unsustainable, Global Leaders Recommit to Joint Climate Action, at Opening of Stockholm Summit," United Nations, June 2, 2022, https://press.un.org/en/2022/envdev2046.doc.htm.

10 R. Ziatdinov and J. Cilliers, "Generation Alpha: Understanding the Next Cohort of University Students," *European Journal of Contemporary Education* 10, no. 3 (2021): 783–89.

Chapter 3

Existing business model

The second theme to consider when making changes within a business model is the existing business model itself. As with strategy, it can often be overlooked as the focus is on the deficiencies and issues within the business. However, by looking at how and, importantly, why a model works the way it does, it will allow for harmonization of the old and new as the process of change occurs.

Evaluate existing business model and make improvement in line with strategy

The existing business models of large international companies are affected by how their value is created, what's going on the world, how they are shaped, what key resources are important, how close the customers are, how the organization is structured, and what deliveries take place. We usually say that there are as many models as there are companies and each model has its own strengths and weaknesses. A review is about following the chain from the segment, the customer, how they work, and all the way to the deliveries. A business model should be as safe as an aircraft that is checked and evaluated on an ongoing basis to give the best results. There are not many travelers who would like to fly on a plane that does not complete its list of safety requirements, in the same way that it is not effective for customers to purchase from a company who suffers from constant bottlenecks in a production that is lacking for various reasons.

It is not uncommon for international companies to have their customer in one country and produce in a number of other countries with internal actors and external partners.[1] It may be that the company has a customer who orders industrial parts in Amsterdam with delivery timeframe in six months. Some are manufactured in the Netherlands, for example the casing, and the other contents are produced in several other countries. There may be complications in the details that make the company train sister companies or subcontractors and later also undergo quality control in that

DOI: 10.4324/9781003402121-3

country where the parts are produced. The leadership does not want the company to stock more than necessary on site but prefers larger container deliveries and that the warehousing is done in the producing country due to margins and costs. The companies can have many products running with several different stages in both their own companies and together with others. Entire chains of articles and components can be viewed via business and management systems. The central element is dominated by timely purchasing, quantity, quality, availability of relevant expertise, system support, production capacity, and distribution.

The global world is close to us in everything from products to services. We live together and consume food, clothes, and insights from many places every day without really knowing where they are from. It is fascinating and scary at the same time. We have come to understand that the different activities in a business model, which later turn into a chain of events and create a business model, can be complex, difficult to overview, and require extensive research. An overview takes time, but our view is that it always creates added value, especially if the model is exposed to clear external driving forces. It is incredibly important to take the right road to get onto the highway of an efficient and productive business. There are great benefits to doing this mapping before a business model innovation project to identify minor improvements and bottlenecks. For companies, it can also create an awareness and a good platform for future work on a project, but it also means that a larger project can be put to the side and be further evaluated at a later time.

A larger group had many operations throughout the whole country and there had been requests from several customers to be able to buy the more qualified services and with centralized purchases because the needs existed nationally and internationally. The various operations, which were companies in companies, had their own agreements with the larger customers and also their own local consultants plus a large group of partners.

A reorganization was judged to be too risky and costly in the first step. To strengthen relations, the company decided to initially conduct an internal review of its business model, and then consider an alternative model for the delivery of its services. In the first step, as an alternative, they offered their own internal controller who gathered agreements, consultants, and partners in one solution.

They conducted their own internal study and anchored the healthy process on a number of occasions. Customers bought more and after another year a new study was conducted and a reorganization was carried out to the regions. The large customer who asked for the change did not buy as much as the change progressed, so instead the strategy was shifted to another segment internationally.

We believe that a company can gain a lot from an early understanding of customer segmentation, deep customer value, and prioritizing their relationships. There are many questions about how to create value in business models within all parts to get the best interconnections in these activities. It can be an advantage if each activity has unique properties that facilitate the anchoring of understanding. Many times, it is the ignorance that contributes to the formation of bottlenecks and the lack of strategies. If the chain of activities is not clear, it also becomes difficult to create different strategies for all parts and the overall solution becomes weak. It is important to identify the business chain and how all parties interact and cooperate with each other.

Our experience is that companies like to work with goals, but that reconciliations tend to be about other alternatives in many companies. These points serve as bus stops on the way to the end destination and are the primary source of creating value in a business model. It is about developing the different activities and being able to deepen, improve, and offer something better. If the reconciliations are not made in step with each other, there is an obvious risk that the company's deliveries will end up out of step. Reconciliations are therefore an important parameter in existing models and should be noted during a review.

> The midsize company had changed their manager a number of times in recent years, and with each change, it meant a deterioration in structure, meetings, and common agendas. The existing business had also begun to target a second segment with completely different deliveries.
>
> Some of the company's key employees had therefore left, citing that their work had been eroded and the big jobs could no longer be done. There was now a lack of calculation support, engineers, project managers, and quality monitoring.
>
> The company decided to start a business model innovation project with early meetings. This led to a study with larger customers to understand more about the existing relationships and the delivered value, gather input on their perception, map out where the knowledge was not sufficient, and reintroduce a business model with goals and reconciliations.

The business model depends on trust, transparency, willingness to create together, and that all parties are prepared to clarify every day. It contains many decisions and therefore every minor decision becomes important. For many, this comes as a total surprise when we have knowledge-developing seminars in implementation. If a model is to create value, it is important to have clear agreements with the customer at the start and to have everyone involved by the end in order to achieve world-class deliveries. We are very keen to find and understand agreements and who has been empowered to make decisions.

A fairly common occurrence is that newer management delivers more on its own perceptions than the original agreements as they aren't as bound by them. It can create major problems with customers if it is to their detriment but can also be met with total silence if it is to their advantage. Regardless of which situations management changes in their business models or what motives are at play, these need to be done with corrected agreements. This may involve substantially large margin losses that cannot later be compensated for by higher prices or that more resources in inventory management were required that the customer required for the delivery to be carried out earlier. Management needs to be informed about old decisions that are central to deliveries. The history of the company's deliveries must be understood before any changes are implemented to make sure that there are improvements from the customer perspective.

The international group had had a fantastic development for many years but the growth in several companies was nearly too fast. Several of the subsidiaries had a rate close to or over 100 percent over the past two years; several department managers had switched roles to other departments and the organization changed overall. They were many smaller decisions that were naturally decentralized but several decisions were centralized.

The company with the fastest growth had weekly meetings on Friday afternoons where each department gathered and went through the week and gradually frustration increased because some decisions made deliveries more difficult. The company carried out an internal follow-up and ensured the managers' mandate from the current customer agreements.

The meeting on Friday was scheduled for Mondays on four different occasions so that all department heads could attend the others' meetings. They were carried out on a rolling schedule and documented with responsibility and authority. It was a short-term success, which also contributed to several quality improvements and corrected better prices for the products.

The existing business model may suffer from changed decisions of owners that have not been implemented, management who has not understood the meaning of the board's decision or other reasons for the management fulfilling the decisions such as meeting resistance, having a different view or timing. Often these consequences of decisions are linked to learned behaviors that do not change due to the fact that the partners do not want to incorporate change, cannot change, or have misunderstood what is being asked of them. Even improvements to an existing business model are dependent on behaviors, directly or indirectly. For the manager who understands this quickly at the outset, the result often comes faster.

Insights for evaluating existing business model and make improvements in line with strategy

1. Acknowledge ignorance and where understanding differs
2. Reconciliations are important for creating value
3. Make identifications of early agreements and inventory
4. Management must be informed about old agreements
5. Identify central behaviors around central decisions for the model

Create time for development

The major changes in the 1900s have often been rapid and driven by different countries' ambitions to create competitive advantages. The period as a whole is a milestone in human history with other possibilities in transportation, communication, and natural sciences. It has brought forth new ways for business models to create value by being able to see nations, people, and business with the same binoculars. In the natural sciences, the development of new drugs such as penicillin has certainly contributed to a higher average age and, just as the Internet has done for information, the discovery of the molecular structure of DNA, the cornerstone of life, is a fantastic success.[2] The overall average age in the developed countries increased from an average age of about 60 years at the beginning of the 1900s to 80 years at present, and it has continued to increase.

After World War II, the focus was on dismantling trade barriers, tariffs, and other regulations that limited the conditions for future world trade. The United States supported this effort with Marshall Aid, which could keep up with the demand, and to administer this, the Organization for European Economic Co-operation was created, which later became the Organization for Economic Cooperation and Development in 1960. Initially this group consisted of the United States and Canada and later it grew to include Japan, Australia, along with other members. As early as 1947, the General Agreement on Tariffs and Trade was created, which simplified world trade, and thus bilateral agreements could be introduced or negotiated. Later the agreement became the WTO. It was an agreement that gradually became an organization.[3]

Emerging needs associated with the construction of cities and technologies improved opportunities for developing industries. New industry areas with transport blossomed, and trains could now work to help shipping evolve from simply transporting goods to also transporting people into the ports of the big cities. Countries gradually became dependent on internationalization at a rapid pace, and by the end of the century, people were transported in buses to large shopping centers outside the city centers. Families drive their own cars to their summer houses for recreation and the holidays are expanded and legislated with salary in many Western countries from two weeks to five weeks; for example, two weeks of holiday became statutory in Sweden as early as 1938.[4] The United States still doesn't have statutory leave, but many companies still choose to include between ten and fifteen days into employment contracts.

The medium and large companies have been and continue to be very focused on productivity and identify targets with different ways of measuring. When reviewing the existing business model, it is important to be thorough and map and get to know the situation early on. It is equally important to carry out an assessment of opportunities and risks and provide the project with an equivalent of its own train carriage with interesting and important knowledge that can travel through on interesting trips at the company's stops to toward the destination. A business is much more about getting closer to the customer's needs, creating space for change, and it starts with time and space. Globalization has helped to make the changes feel closer but also removed some of the perception of space.

> The company was a growing midsize group that had developed methods to ensure how best to research and understand their upcoming customers' decisions to purchase their products. They knew that the value was to be found in being able to buy at a reasonable price and that customers' attributes could add value for them.
>
> The entire development of the business model needed more time to ensure the right customers, the right management was in process, and the right understanding of the creation of upcoming residential areas was in place. Gradually, they built companies to manage all important components, from owning land, developing platforms for technology, building, and managing.
>
> It made large early investments in knowledge development studies and data management and initiated meetings to ensure the right areas. In order to grow further, they decided to follow the business along a narrower path and develop a more open climate with customers, which meant that the purchases could be made with an open budget and the profits from it were divided 50 percent each.

We see that the analysis process requires proximity to the questions around which segments need evaluation, in-depth knowledge of behaviors and with the understanding that with more actors change also takes longer. Based on the expected customer value and need, it is easier to create a business model that can deliver world-class products and services. Time is as important to this creation as it is to the train that transports people and goods. For example, if the train misses the time, travelers and freight owners get angry. For an existing business format, there is often a great challenge in understanding and ensuring the accuracy of the needs that create value throughout the chain.

We have long recommended setting aside internal time for review of the business model on an ongoing basis including strategies and ideally an action plan. The team can support with this activity when we have entire projects and study the model in more detail. The internal time can vary with specific orientations such as customers, value, production, resources, and income/costs. It is encouraged that the team feels free to use previous knowledge and changes and compare these against the current situation. It creates new understanding and can help to set a target forward in the future with relevant and focused activities.

The family business had evolved from a small business to a medium-sized group under the father's leadership. The last 30 years had meant a strong increase in larger flows of income and the father's good customer contacts were widely known. There were two children who could carry on the tradition.

To ensure the structure, a conversion work was initiated that clarified the customer process, improved the agreements, clarified the channels, increased service, and secured all deliveries. The father was careful that all customer contacts should be handled carefully and that external help was needed to strengthen the company's structural capital.

The company carried out a three-year process of successive improvements together with us, and at the end of it, the youngest daughter began working in the business. We focused primarily on the fact that the daughter would be able to step into a more finished structure and that the company's strategies would also be clarified throughout the company's business model. The transition was very careful, slow. and profitable. After almost seven years, she became CEO, replacing her father who then transitioned to operate as chairman of the board.

In the change projects, it is important to map the value created in customer relationships and ideally to be able to measure a development through deliveries. When we later conduct troubleshooting seminars after the qualitative studies, the project spends time on the entire value chain where the team members identify potential improvement projects. The companies normally prefer when they can measure customer value and gain more knowledge about what needs the customer demands to be met. If the deliveries hit above or below the expected quality and delivery at the customer level, both situations can lead to falling margins and smaller profits. It is about deepening the understanding by analyzing and agreeing on the real need.

The midsize industry company had shared leadership with a CEO who was responsible for the development of the business and a sales manager who handled segmentation, customer development, channel planning, and customer value. They were equally large partners and had a very close and cooperative relationship between each other and the customers.

When the sales manager suffered a brain hemorrhage and they understood that the effects would remain, they decided to carry out a change project for almost two years with the motivation to later sell the company to a larger player. The two managers did not see that it would work to recruit a replacement; instead they wanted to try to find an external buyer.

The company conducted initial meetings, mapping, an extensive customer study, management seminars, and later also ten customer seminars. Three years after the incident, the company was successfully sold after creating even better customer value, increasing sales, and developing a nice profit. The sale was also adapted to what the buying company needed.

It is often a very creative process to go through an existing business model that requires planning, mapping, and time. We see this initial process as a necessary feasibility study before a qualitative study and know that the time can vary from days, weeks to a few years. Most people still choose to proceed with a deeper and more extensive renovation. As with a company that isn't operating as well as it has in the past, the driving forces that created a train's misalignment or derailment need to be mapped and corrected. Perhaps it is the case that the main line or gears were worn down and eventually needed to be replaced.

Our view is that management often determines the conditions more than others as to whether it will be a good review or not. Most organizations know their bottlenecks but few want to make managers aware of what is actually happening. It can be about a resistance of attitude that will negatively affect the organizational structure, the decision-making structure, or the personal relationships. An additional detail is that the leader may have a lack of time right from the start and then the project will also be insecure as it progresses.

Insights for creating time for development

1. Understanding and ensuring the accuracy of the needs
2. Internal time for review of the business model
3. Map the value created in customer relationships
4. Creative process that requires planning, mapping, and time
5. Management often determines the conditions (step back)

Anchor with owner, management, and the organization

In today's medium and large companies, technological development continues both internally with various systems that help the company to handle administration, information, communication, planning and externally in developing new innovations in products and services. It is many hundreds of years back that the Spinning Jenny and steam engine were developed in the United Kingdom during the 1700s.[5] Many of today's new technologies are also further developments from the electrification of the 1900s, the internal combustion engine, transport, and the emergence of the entire computer field. In the 1700s, the new technologies replaced professions and industries while the development of the past hundred years has created many new professions and technologies.

The current trend of computerization has been very much to replace jobs and it has and will continue to affect business models, but we also see that it often creates growth and it can be about a lack of knowledge and having enough machines.[6] The technical aids with AI at the forefront will have a hard time replacing creativity and the social interactions that exists between humans but the evolving tools like ChatGPT (Generative Pre-Trained Transformer) will simplify most tasks, and it is important to ask what we can best use it for.[7] All of these technological innovations reduce barriers to creating products and services, which leads to increased competition and generally lower prices as more people get access to the new devices and software. Generative AI is likely to contribute to more creative professions but with a negative impact on wage growth within these groups.

Today, management is expected to have more prior knowledge and the staffs of the larger companies are decreasing in line with the availability of data and technology. At the same time, we see a trend that the expected prior knowledge does not always exist, and controlling only with data is more difficult because the companies are still made up of people.[8] These risks are giving birth to internal informal decision-making systems in some companies, especially among those who do not have majority shareholders. A CEO with responsibility for 100 companies in 60 countries finds it more difficult to really know what is happening on the ground in the companies. A countervailing effect that we have seen in recent years is that more companies work more deeply with authorizations. At the same time, there may be cultural and legal differences between countries as to what are possible decisions to authorize certain practices within the organization. When business models change, there needs to be a foothold with those who own the issues regardless.

A medium-sized international company with strong growth focused on consumer-related products and services had difficulty anchoring the

*decisions of owners, management, and down to the various depart-
ments. The company felt that they had difficulty developing their internal
division of labor with responsibility, authority, and control.*

*The acute lack of time was linked to more products, the amount of
business, and a doubling of the number of employees. This meant that
the previous informal structure instead hampered overview, feedback,
and implementation of necessary changes. They decided to start an
innovation work project aimed at creating a better management structure with clearer frameworks and boundaries to take better care of skills
and develop the necessary knowledge.*

*A completely new segment emerged as a result of the initial meetings,
which turned into a really successful outcome. The work went on for
two years with a qualitative study, an improved business organization
with more levels of decisions, and follow-up studies. The implemented
changes brought renewed strength, increased growth in revenue and
sales, and a margin improvement.*

There is an absolute need for anchoring the existing business model, understanding how customer value is created and how it should be developed
from owners, the board, and management. We believe that the larger
companies need to allocate more resources to acquire knowledge about
the market, segments, and the opportunities available and create a better
consensus. We see the old stories that all international markets are local
and require local expertise and these have changed over time in line with
technological development. The insights and decisions are likely to change
even more as today's younger leaders take the lead in the larger companies
because of their freer approach to empowerment and the power of various
tools in data.

Technological development enables faster access to fact-based decisions, but it also poses a great challenge not to be too quick on the needs
of certain customer groups. Our experience shows that companies rather
need more research to decipher data and that this expertise is emerging at
the same time as many experts in fields are reporting that it is not possible
to trust the content of all data. There can be false positives and negatives,
missing datasets or simply a lack of interpretation which could lead to erro-
neous decision-making. It is therefore crucial to ensure that time is taken
to analyze the available data and run it through several key people before
presenting it as a platform from which to launch decision-making.

*An international industrial company had acute problems with wide-
spread dissatisfaction directed at an unclear owner and a management
team with no real power to act. Resistance had spread over the past
two years mainly related to the management of acquisitions and the*

different corporate cultures but also with underdeveloped decision-making systems.

The previously open organization allowed active involvement in all matters, something that had instead become a brake on growth. The lack of clear boundaries, information management, and middle managers instead led to speculation. This was occurring at the same time as the larger customers continued to order, and the development began to affect customer value and deliveries.

The owners and the board of directors decided to carry out a review of the company's strategies and then map out the current business model. We started one-to-one meetings for a year and made successive improvements by gathering staff on an ongoing basis in work meetings. We then conducted a qualitative study, internal and external, which gave a positive outcome and several subsequent management seminars.

An increased insight into the development of customer value in a business model can serve as a security for profitable customer groups, new possible segments, channel choices, and how the company creates a secure value development together with its key customers. The local anchoring in international companies is important, above all, for the development of customer relationships and for knowing what the unique activities look like locally. International innovation is often about ensuring better skills in another country and thus also a contribution to distributing the risk better for an entire solution.

The previously implemented change in the business model had not worked painlessly in the large international industrial company. The production was managed with a centralized management but there were different production solutions in several different locations. The difficulties were mainly due to undeveloped support systems and the fact that the local managers felt that they were not given enough time to return feedback.

An improvement was needed where the solution also offered better opportunities to control for local needs with managers more involved in the customer process, which would speed up decisions and motivate employees.

To handle the situation, they conducted a business model innovation process over two years. The internal behavioral changes had rapid positive effects and contributed to better customer management and a number of improvements in product development.

An anchoring process is a social process between owners, board, and management, which focuses on the company's opportunities in selected customer areas and on how an improved creation of customer value can contribute to continued success for the company. These are complex processes that require those involved to be prepared to work with common agreements, as compromise is a natural feature of any agreement. The joint agreements have many difficulties, but the benefits are also great in being able to implement short-term improvements to the business model or longer, more extensive changes. Our experience shows that the expectations of economic effects contribute to the different images and these in turn usually depend on which internal or external driving forces are relevant to start a project. In these cases, applied research can offer a tool for an improved common process to parties who are involved in both the organization on a regular basis and a decision to implement a business model innovation project.

Insights for anchoring with the owner, management, and the organization

1. Understand the business model and how customer value is created.
2. Faster access to fact-based decisions.
3. Increased insight into the development of customer value.
4. Local anchoring in international companies is important.
5. Social process between owners, board, and management.

Clarify and understand customer value – safety, delivery, and avoiding problems

Many of the new technologies can change status although they are also a further development of old techniques. It creates new opportunities for several of these developments and alternative revenue streams. For companies, this means that the external driving forces increase, and customer value must be followed more than before so that they can be analyzed, developed, and ensured.[9] Changing use of services and products is faster in today's society than yesterday, but at the same time, we see that many companies have become better at following early signals. There is still a major challenge in interpreting the existing amount of data, which has also increased for most companies and with them it also serves as an actual basis for decision-making. The risk of confusion between data and what is actually measured is great, just as for humans the risk increases without movement and it is important to continue to move forward.

There are many perceptions of customer value and technological developments that have enabled more measurement than before. The traditional view is that the key thing is the benefit that companies deliver and it has two dimensions, the desired benefit and the delivered benefit. To understand the value, the customer needs to be involved, and there are several variants of studies that can offer satisfied customer indices.[10] Many times, leaders make decisions based on past experiences, subjective perceptions, and generational mindsets. What companies can influence in their range of products and services is quality, usability, desired characteristics, cost, and even image. There are often great opportunities with a more flexible approach when analyzing the existing business model and at the same time many behavioral obstacles along the way stand to be understood and negotiated.

The rapid development in information and communication also opens up the possibility that the companies need to review routines for how the flow should work with e-mail, the Internet, social platforms, conferences, and other meeting places. The better companies have more frequent contact at all levels of a business solution and try to be proactive and run faster than their customers to better anticipate their needs. It also measures more frequent customer indices quantitatively, which helps to see bottlenecks earlier and then be able to understand more deeply with qualitative interviews or focus groups. For us, the trend is clear that the technological tools have created greater proximity between people and influenced the feeling between time and space. The customer value is like a long-distance race where the runner's results are dependent on previous training, sleep, and replenishment of energy before and during the race. What we can learn from different situations is that the results are usually dependent on preparation, analyses, exercises, tests, and controls in implementation.

The large company was the market leader and had its great focus on being involved in developing within their country and with international knowledge outreach in a larger market. Over the previous ten years, the company had conducted quantitative studies with a satisfied customer index and made successive improvements for its customers based on these answers.

They were a larger company with over 500 employees and felt that their organization was not really adapted to what customers increasingly demanded. They decided to implement a business innovation model process by clarifying a purpose and conducting a comprehensive qualitative study.

The idea was to get closer by getting qualitative views from the company's most important customers. These could more directly provide views on the brand, customer orientation and contribute to strengthening the customer offering going forward. The results were later a change in the company's organization that could more easily follow, create, and develop customer value. It later resulted in a new business solution with a widened strategy and a new customer organization.

Through a large number of projects, we have been able to establish that an important success factor is that the companies that succeed better spend more time deepening their understanding of customer behavior. We also see that several larger companies are gathering internal services in revenue, pricing, customer relation marketing (CRM), and search engine optimization. It often involves trying to understand and further align needs with attributes by gaining access to how customers make detailed decisions.

In order to develop better, it is beneficial to try to understand how the value of customer benefit can be ensured in a process, then create alternative proposals to the current solution, and explain how it should be structured within the different steps. We have seen that the work needs to include how the processes are affected in parts and the whole as well and that the key resources need to be identified and compared with the previous use in established processes.

The softer part of the customer benefit should not be underestimated in terms of brand and image for both parties. In business model innovation, we look not only for the value of the services and products but also for uniqueness and that the chain should preferably not be duplicated by their competitors. A strong product may also be added to its own consumable inventory items, which then means increased sales but above all that the unique products have other aspects in their solution that create ongoing additional revenue.

They were a major medium-sized service company with a focus on designing and developing expensive products. The company's focus gradually strengthened as products and services became more solid and the business process was perceived to be stable enough.

The various elements were analyzed carefully before becoming an important part of the delivery of the entire chain and at the same time initial investments were required to develop the company's products. It was a difficult balancing act, but through increased market knowledge, a clear tough subscription and, above all, early customer contacts, relationships could develop positively and a clear value emerged.

The owner decided to increase the understanding of its products regarding the quality, making a cost estimate for usability and developing an image around the total delivery of the entire product. They also linked external support for their innovation development with qualitative customer studies, external contacts, and knowledge of market. Very little was left to chance.

The expected value and the perceived value need to be ensured in order for the quality to match what the customer later receives. When we conduct follow-up seminars from the studies and develop different projects within the business model, value is always one of the most discussed items. It is just as often about the start of the relationship and what the initial agreements actually mean as problem issues related to the deliveries. It is crucial to make a general inventory of the value and at the same time study the entire side of potential and actual income and costs to the products and/or services. We call that exercise the security classification of the possibilities; they can be valued from one to five.

In striving to find an alignment in the expected and perceived values through a general inventory, it provides the opportunity to look at the reality of where a company is operating from prior to embarking on making changes within a business model. Depending on the status of how decisions are made, the data available and the veracity of the analysis of information form a multi-angle look at the values of a company, which ensures that the management can get closer what the customer can expect from the company. This in turn increases the predictive ability for the end-user of the products and services on offer before, during, and after a change process.

The company was in need of control because they had several very different operations with large demanding customer groups. The overall business model was to deliver world-class services in the field of service and nursing. They felt that quality was the big challenge and in the collective agreements they were forced into certain guarantees that could be difficult to deliver on and, above all, understand.

They decided to conduct a larger study in several customer segments and then conduct focus groups together with customers. It would give them further knowledge of how the offer could develop and also be able to answer which driving forces could be important now and in the long run.

In these meetings, they were able to trim their offerings, ensure the guarantees through a better common understanding, and also ensure that the management would be able to control and lead more securely. A big benefit of the projects was that it allowed cross-functional leadership, and thus the leaders could get more perspectives on their respective customer groups.

We see the value questions as important pieces of the puzzle to be able to offer products and services that have clear business models. Developing understanding of value can be controlled with algorithms and obtaining clear streams of information can highlight which attributes customers prefer. The alternative is to do deep customer studies and then focus groups that act as test groups. It is central to test the value so as not to end up with the wrong conclusion and deliver on an expected value that later turns out to be completely incorrect. We see the whole idea of testing faster and following the value development as a clear success factor for the best companies – they test and can correct on the fly.

Insights for clarifying and understanding customer value

1. Deepening their understanding of customer behavior
2. Clear customer value benefit to a better process
3. Search for unique value
4. Make a general inventory of the value
5. Use test of value from throughout the value chain

Communicate easily and a lot – regularly for understanding and with follow-ups

The spread of information has exploded over the past century, and communication has been possible through telegraph stations, gramophones, telephones, radio and television, mobiles, and of course the Internet for more than 25 years.[11] There have been many different external and internal driving forces behind this extraordinary development, but the common thing that drives this evolution is that we are social beings who want to investigate, challenge, and understand each other. Communication contains thoughts, feelings, and experiences and therefore is extraordinarily important when we want to create a change in behaviors in ourselves and together with others.[12] We can turn and twist the words, relate to the body, and not least use our voice.

Global growth in recent years has taken a hit from the pandemic and subsequent conflicts in various parts of the world. However, the future is expected to continue with technological growth in the immediate and longer term with a two-sided effect, with emerging markets increasing with China, India, and Indonesia and the fast-growing countries Turkey, Mexico, and Vietnam increasing their importance. Emerging markets have a clear focus on also improving and developing institutions and infrastructure. In the shorter term, development will focus more on machine learning, AI, robot processing, and edge computing. Knowledge is an important area for medium and large companies both to be able to adapt their organizations and to understand the future in order to be able to recruit better.

The business models of larger companies require proactive communication because there are usually more people involved and a mix between the parent organization and other partners. More nuanced communication is required, which is explained more where everyone involved can and is expected to seek their own information via internal systems. We have noticed that partner training has become more important and that the development, with on-call services, complaints departments, and fast service, has increased. A number of companies that we have worked with have also integrated both forward and backward in the value chain and completed acquisitions to offer a more comprehensive model with other services deemed important in the future. The big gain for the business model is to carry out successive follow-ups and communicate the result to everyone involved to make progress. Most people who are going to build a new house ensure that the construction techniques are best suited for the site. They do not build a dry foundation on a marshland but use piles if the house is to survive and be worth the investment.

An international conglomerate gradually built up a larger company in infrastructure and frequently bought companies with interesting products and also invested in research in certain product groups. It was primarily an investment in labs and factories with unique solutions and products that would be communicated through various distributor chains around the world.

The investments were heavy in product development, but they also had an international marketing and sales organization that conveyed the messages to prescribing consultants, distributors, and even end customers who bought large orders from other partners.

To strengthen its solution in the Nordic region, it conducted a survey with business model innovation aimed at identifying the needs of the different channels and being able to both develop the right products but also to sharpen its external communication. The innovative project lasted for almost three years with a gradual development of unique solutions and changes in the existing business solution.

Internal and external communication is an important instrument for growth and harmonizing human behavior. In this, there is a major task when customer benefit is to be analyzed and developed in an existing business model. We have gained an amazing insight into how difficult and challenging it can be to actually understand and follow a value for the companies' customers. This derives from our 1,500 seminars with management since the beginning of this work and how we have developed tools to help interpret messages, relationships, and situations. More seminars are often needed that can develop common images of what is important for following processes and introducing follow-up that can be measured.

When we conduct reviews of existing business models, we both look behind data and search for whether our client conducts regular meetings with their customers where they focus on the business model and its effects. If it does not exist before an innovation project, we recommend that they introduce this practice before the project begins and ensure that there is a follow-up in place. There is a great advantage to let the customer gain insight and contribute to better processes both for the efficiency of the model but also to be able to cost proof much of what actually happens. For an upcoming project, this means an opportunity for reconciliations and easier access to questions and answers.

The international company had several different services for leisure and development. They were a larger player with several different businesses that would geographically collaborate even if they had differentiated customers and value creation. In recent years, occupancy had increased significantly while it was a challenge to develop leaders and retain key personnel. Some of the operations were also more resource-intensive, which affected motivation throughout the company.

There was also some concern that some major customer agreements would be affected going forward if the development were to continue in the wrong direction. In order to solve the questions in the short term, it created a forum for the company's most important customer groups, which helped the company to make successive improvements. The overall goal provided an opportunity to respond to the short-term need of the business.

The starting point for the initial meetings was to improve and develop understanding of customer needs with a focus on deliveries. They did a review in several different steps with a focus on improving and developing business, creating value and clarifying how communication should best be built and in which channels. The project included studies, various seminars, and focus groups for more central messages.

The initial reviews focus on how the company communicates and which channels are used for different activities. We can see that this often serves as a mirror to the management that leads the company. There is an interest in transparency, and to share more, the communication is usually more developed and vice versa. Internal communication often begins directly upon employment with various information to be communicated between the employee and the employer. Many larger companies call it onboarding just like when we get on an airplane with a predetermined location, thus creating a way to ensure that the right conditions are in place for the passenger with a boarding pass who boards the company's journey. What's different is that the company cannot tell you the exact flight time, crew, flight route (depending on weather), and destination. However, the best companies spend more time ensuring that all are valuable in creating value, and it helps how we are received and taken care of and how relationships

develop. We make important initial agreements that are confirmed with a
boarding activity.

> *The medium-sized company had lost part of its identity as the parent
> company had created new services to be performed alongside their own
> and preferably with the same business model. There were daily problems
> around internal communication in everything from orders to deliveries
> due to different perceptions of the different importance of the services.*
>
> *Despite the problems, the company still created growth with good
> results, and the management judged that it was a matter of time before
> the company could not deliver customer value to its existing customers
> to the same extent because the employees had double assignments that
> were also very different in deliveries.*
>
> *The initial focus was to solve the questions on the value-creating
> activities of the various services and redistribute better to reduce risks.
> The work continued with a combination study with employees and cus-
> tomers. This led to new overall management and two business areas.
> The internal information and communication were strengthened via a
> number of joint company meetings with hundreds of participants and
> the external via focus groups.*

It is important to understand how the information and communication will
support the business model when the initial review is carried out and later
built on as a project. If there is a lack of communication or certain strategies that can be refined in an existing model, it should be done before a
major project. It can be done by harmonizing certain overall messages: a
customer magazine that will come out every quarter that is now coming out
ad hoc; a logotype that should be blue but has four different colors because
three different printing houses have been used; and most recently in the
company's own copier was enlisted for the job or that more employees
have added their own images and more cool typography to their e-mails,
meaning they have left the company's design program. Without clear and
consistent communication at all levels, any improvement project that may
be undertaken will have significant challenges to overcome before any real
growth can take place, which is why it is essential that this piece of the puzzle is addressed prior to moving forward in an innovation process.

Insights for communicating easily and often

1. Inventory of all communications and behaviors
2. Planning of information and communication channels
3. Analyzed and developed customer value
4. Unified message with images, sounds, and written words
5. Regular follow-up meetings with customers

Summary

When embarking on any kind of project that can lead to changes, whether they are large full-scale processes or more localized tweaks to trim and streamline a business, taking time to really explore and understand the business model and its component parts will allow for more specific work and predictable results. Rather than simply looking at what the business is, doing a systematic breakdown of various aspects of how the pieces go together in a company means that the project can have more dynamic elements and allow for understanding of what the project may entail.

At the outset, looking at the business model in detail will reveal areas of ignorance and where understanding differs within the organization. Once this is done, reconciliations can be made, which will be important for creating value. As part of this process, it is not just the current business that needs to be understood but also identifying the early agreements that have been made and ensuring that the management is fully aware of the provenance and nature of those agreements. Once this is done, the areas of the strategies that suffer from the changes in decisions by the owners can be highlighted and addressed, along with identifying the target behaviors on the central decisions for the model. By taking time to investigate and understand where the business model comes from as well as how it is functioning at present, it will allow for the changes that are proposed to either enhance or replace current processes and functions within the model.

It can be an exciting time when embarking on change but a huge key to the success of an innovation project is to take time for the development. The scale may well change depending on the needs of the company and depths of the issues to be addressed. The great challenge is in understanding and ensuring the accuracy of the needs and then setting aside internal time for a review of the business model on an ongoing basis, which should include strategies and ideally an action plan. It is important to map the value created in customer relationships and preferably to be able to measure development through deliveries. There is a creative element in the process of going through an existing business model that requires planning, mapping, and time, and generally speaking, it is the management that often determines the conditions more than others whether it will be a good review or not.

As with other parts of business model innovation, it is essential to anchor each phase with the owner, the management, and the organization. The need is absolute to anchor the business model and how the customer value is created. It can often be easy to move very quickly with faster access to information to create fact-based decisions, but this also poses a great challenge to not be too quick based on the needs of a certain customer. By really rooting the understanding of the existing business model, it will provide increased insight into the development of customer value, and as the world continues to become smaller due to technological advances, it is easier to acknowledge the importance of local anchoring in international companies. A key thing to always keep in mind is that this kind of project isn't simply data-driven but is truly a social process between owners, board members, and management about the company's opportunities, and while agreements can have many difficulties, the benefits are also great.

Placing customer value in the spotlight of interrogating an existing business model will allow for great clarification and understanding of customer value. Companies succeed better when they spend more time deepening their understanding of customer behavior. They also acknowledge how the value of customer benefit can be ensured throughout the process, often by bringing together value with uniqueness in their products and services while ensuring that their chain of procedures are not easily replicated by their competitors. The perspective can be radically shifted by this customer-centered approach, at which point a general inventory of the value must be made and include a process of testing the value so as to not come to incorrect conclusions, which will lead to delivery on an incorrect expected value.

During the excavation of an existing business model and as the innovation process continues it is essential that communication happens easily and often. When done consistently, internal and external communications are important instruments for growth and harmonizing human behavior. It is a major task when customer benefit is analyzed and developed so it is also important to develop common images of what is important for following processes and to introduce a system of following up. It is key to place the customer at the center of this process, and so it is key to conduct regular meetings with customers where the focus is the business model and its effects as there is a great advantage in letting the customer gain insight and contribute better to the processes.

The initial reviews at this stage focus on how the company communicates and which channels are used for different activities, and going forward it is important to understand how the information and communication will support the business model. If it is clear that there is a lack of communication or certain strategies can be refined in an existing model, this is something that should be taken care of before working on a major project.

The process of getting to the core of an existing business model is an essential and often interesting part of the process of beginning a project of change. Not only is the information that is discovered necessary to the further evolution of the company, but it is an opportunity to understand the blueprint of where the organization comes from. It is often enlightening to follow current processes and procedures back to the situation that caused the decision to be made in the first place. Where this can be understood, it is invaluable to creating the plans and maps for future change.

Notes

1 Peter Vanham, "A Brief History of Globalization," *Geo Economics, World Economic Forum*, January 17, 2019, https://www.weforum.org/agenda/2019/01/how-globalization-4-0-fits-into-the-history-of-globalization/.

2 American Chemical Society International Historic Chemical Landmarks, "Discovery and Development of Penicillin," http://www.acs.org/content/acs/en/education/whatischemistry/landmarks/flemingpenicillin.html.

3 Tom Petersson, *History of Swedish Business 1864–2014, del IV: 1965–1985* (Stockholm: Dialogos Förlag, 2014).

4 Samuel Greén, "Summer Vacation Has Not Always Been Obvious," *forskning.se.*, July 22, 2013, https://www.forskning.se/2013/07/22/sommarledighet-har-inte-alltid-varit-sjalvklart/.

5 R. C. Allen, "The Industrial Revolution in Miniature: The Spinning Jenny in Britain, France, and India," *The Journal of Economic History* 69, no. 4 (2009): 901–27.

6 James Bessen, "How Computer Automation Affects Occupations: Technology, Jobs, and Skills," Centre for Economic Policy Research, September 22, 2016, https://cepr.org/voxeu/columns/how-computer-automation-affects-occupations-technology-jobs-and-skills.

7 Christian Stadler and Martin Reeves, "Chatting About Strategy: The Uses and Limits of Large Language Models," BCG Henderson Institute, March 2, 2023, https://bcghendersoninstitute.com/chatting-about-strategy/.

8 Marcy Farrell, "Data and Intuition: Good Decisions Need Both," Harvard Business Publishing Corporate Learning, January 6, 2023, https://www.harvardbusiness.org/data-and-intuition-good-decisions-need-both/.

9 J. Barland, "Innovation of New Revenue Streams in Digital Media: Journalism as Customer Relationship," *Nordicom Review* 34, no. S1 (2013): 99–112.

10 A. Graf and P. Maas, "Customer Value from a Customer Perspective: A Comprehensive Review," *Journal für Betriebswirtschaft* 58, no. 1 (2008): 1–20.

11 Kevin Webb, "From the Internet to the iPhone, Here Are the 20 Most Important Inventions of the Last 30 Years," *Insider*, May 17, 2019, https://www.businessinsider.com/most-important-inventions-of-last-30-years-internet-iphone-netflix-facebook-google-2019-5?op=1&r=US&IR=T.

12 P. Salovey and J. D. Mayer, "Emotional Intelligence," *Imagination, Cognition, and Personality* 9, no. 3 (1990): 185–211, Sage Publications Inc.

Chapter 4

Customer orientation

The third theme to take in as part of changing a business model is customer orientation. Customers are the lifeblood of a company, and it is critical to understand not only who they are but also how they connect and interact with the organization. Taking the time and using all available tools to assess the relationship a business has to their customers will allow for growth and strengthening future relationships.

Direct toward energizing and developing business

The global market has given companies greater opportunities to broaden their business models in several countries and also to find material alternatives and sources of revenue.[1] The multinationals have helped to internationalize countries and spread products and goods all over the world. Several important conditions have gradually contributed to the freer flow of possible goods and services, the technological conditions for moving products, and the development of information to be able to communicate faster and reach agreements. Technological development has contributed greatly to the world of business by generating opportunities to meet entrepreneurs and capitalists from all over the world. More people have been able to find alternative segments and customers and build relationships internationally.

The focus on business models has increased dramatically over the past 25 years, and with globalization and market development, interest has increased at the speed of the fastest boat on open water. Technological development has made it possible to easily move directly to the market and search for interesting segments and opportunities. Processing has been simplified through various marketing systems, such as CRM, which can manage and identify customer areas in an easier way than before. Today, customer development can take place between countries in a different way with contacts over e-mail, Microsoft Teams, or other platforms.[2]

For the development of existing business models, the availability of data is important. As data usage increases, there are also more people who point

DOI: 10.4324/9781003402121-4

to customers generally becoming more agile than before. We see that when the winds blow and the changes in the outside world move faster, competition is also distorted and sometimes the spinning winds end up pointing a company completely in the wrong direction. For medium and large companies, this means more focus on key resources but also trying to maintain and develop flexibility to meet new risks. It is important to maintain and develop customer relationships even as business models grow in their solutions with more players, partners, and difficult logistics solutions to eventually assemble and develop the products. In line with this development, companies have moved many customer decisions to management so as not to lose important insight and momentum in customer relationships. It is an exciting development that we are faced with.

> The medium-sized industrial company had been around for a long time in the international markets and regardless of the dominant owner, the company had continued to buy more businesses to add more expertise and build new or strengthen existing segments.
>
> Now the company was facing a name change, which would affect the existing brands more than before. There were those who felt a concern about being linked to a simpler industrial service that existed at the company that set the name. It would be turbulent, according to management, but the owners had made up their minds.
>
> When the name change was carried out, the company that gave the name brought in external consultants to support the process forward and deepen knowledge of the market, segments, existing customer relationships, and how the joint companies could build on alternative channels. An overarching question for the project was whether a new business model could create economies of scale between a number of countries and which key resources would be crucial.

Our view is that interest in different customer groups has strengthened over the past ten years, with an interesting break due to COVID-19 in the last couple of years. Several companies were directly affected by regulations and closed societies while some segments benefited. There are driving forces that have affected working life: hybrid work, alternative ways of traveling, and some signs that many countries' trade has become more local. We have noticed in our last 200 seminars that interest in customer needs has increased and many business leaders find it difficult to make rational decisions. There is an important difference here, when data make it more possible to analyze customers than before, which indirectly affects customer benefit. We see a change in the way of leading companies where part of the control has been moved down to the management that has received greater empowerment and the manager has had to work even more to strengthen the brand than before.

Another factor that affects developing and strengthening of the business is the open society and how companies should seek information, resources, and key competences within a mix between local and international partners. We see that it benefits companies that have an international outlook and they can change faster and find the resources or skills needed faster than their competitors. The combined factors of our themes also benefit those companies that operate in more than two markets, as it is more favorable to develop unique products and dynamic capabilities. Of course, it differs from company to company and it is also to understand what driving forces trigger a change and which alternative structures are possible to develop in and from.

The medium-sized company had grown rapidly over the past five years but now faced several new challenges when the large customer wanted to order more. The customer organization was not in place and the employment in production had increased by almost 100 percent in only the past year, so the limitations of the premises were soon the next challenge.

There was a need for more structure and understanding of the business model and to be more able to make the customer's needs visible in order to develop more unique, smart, and cost-effective solutions. The company decided to take in external help in its growth journey by creating an overall innovation process.

It rather quickly led to a new marketing organization that could follow products and services, ensure internal resources with internal planning for production, and be the project manager through the processes. The company had put the first shovel into the ground in a structure for a customer manager. Growth could continue.

There are great gains in customer management if companies can identify future valuable needs that can be transformed faster than others with a good business model. We see that medium-sized companies often end up with issues that are more about internal obstacles and the organization than creating new business. This also applies to larger companies, but it is mainly old culture that usually puts an end to changes in those organizations. Older leaders are more experienced, often wise, but are also very driven in being managers with stagnant perceptions and very set ways of doing most things. Younger managers have a more open approach to being a manager and share more of the skills that build new knowledge. It feels hopeful for the future and, above all, for continued knowledge development. An important difference is that the younger generation has been interested in available data and sees openness as something more natural than the older generation, which often had to seek answers in several stages to understand.

In recent years, the family business had expanded its customer groups, which had meant a fairly rapid growth from 30 to almost 125 employees.

The old structure of the business model didn't really hang around but it compensated the owners by working smarter and more flexibly. The great asset was the ability to see upcoming needs, develop relationships in the right groups, and create possible new business with creative efforts in new channels.

The company combined the growth with an innovation project aimed at strengthening the business model in the early stages and improving overall decision-making. It progressed at full speed, but there was also a concern that the value-creating activities needed to be planned, controlled, and followed up better.

After setting the purpose an extensive review of the existing business model was carried out and this work led to corrections in communication, continued with a combined customer and staff study, several seminars focused on the new services and profitability of investments made, and the advent of new management meetings. A new manager was hired and the project had external support for three years, more in the beginning and declining as the company's resources were constantly in focus.

It is always exciting when working with a legacy company with a proud history and solid record of success. However, a major challenge is to be able to develop new values over already-existing values, in which there is often a conflict. We have several examples where companies have had very profitable technology but also see that they can sell a cheaper variant to more people. In the short term, it gives a conversion cost and clearly worse margins, but in the long run, they sell to significantly more customers at a lower margin and then the profit comes much later. We see that the driving forces in these larger markets have increased, especially the external ones, and there is a great need for more market knowledge, understanding needs, being able to develop the right channels, trimming the existing solution, creating more joint ventures, testing, and, above all, being positive about new opportunities. It is important to communicate a lot and follow up everything that is possible to follow up to speed up the development of knowledge. The company that does not test will gradually get worse margins. The company that is not focusing on the customer's value will lose the personal relationships and potentially be out of perspective in the business. Most of what we do should be done in just the right way and at the right pace.

Insights for energizing

1. Secure an international outlook
2. Create and inventory of external driving forces
3. Follow and inventory of customer groups
4. Identify future valuable needs and customer management
5. Develop new values over already-existing values

Develop a customer management structure that can justify the investment

The local and international markets act as each other's mirrors where culture, laws, and other incentives both complicate and simplify.[3] One challenge is how companies will transport goods between continents, which is still a matter for container traffic on boats, trucks, planes, and trains. Another challenge is that currency management can shift and countries also prioritize according to their consistent weather patterns or climate, which means that people in colder countries spend more on their homes, winter clothes, winter tires/service on cars, and vice versa. This is compensated through financial systems and is governed by centralized commitments with laws and regulations from country to country. It also differs based on how the general tax bases per country finance different welfare systems in everything from child care and schools, to buses, subways, trains, and roads, right down to retirement and care of the elderly.

A customer segmentation can, at first glance, be quite simple to carry out, but gradually there are more issues that need to be broken down that demonstrably affect the business. It requires an orientation that means that knowledge grows gradually.[4] This style of learning is similar to how people read a daily newspaper, from the beginning or the end. For companies, external knowledge, industry knowledge, and detailed knowledge of what is possible for the company are needed. For international companies that operate in more than two markets, there needs to be an evaluation of resources, skills, and opportunities on an ongoing basis. Above all, companies need to be vigilant for rapid changes in the world around them and be actively prepared for those changes.

Medium and large companies often have customer solutions based on key account management where the customer is managed at different levels with different authorizations to make decisions for that particular level. This type of solution usually also has internal and external analyses to help, but above all it is about the different levels having different responsibilities for the relationships, and at the top it is almost always about the agreement and there you meet less often if everything works. We see that this solution works well, but for a change in a business model, it is better to have a customer manager who leads, identifies bottlenecks, motivates, and develops the business model. It is reminiscent of the traditional role of planning, organizing, staffing, leading, and controlling – but is more focused on the creation, development, and future management of the business.

The large international group had had a tough time in recent years with continued development of its instruments for customers and experienced an improvement every quarter since COVID-19 was over. The customer groups had shifted abruptly, but the group managed to change quickly and managed the economy, thanks to a built-up knowledge of its customers.

The rapid changes of recent years had created a new situation with new insights that indicated that it must be possible to understand customer needs more deeply and be able to keep up with their attributes better. Their services were divided into two main groups where travel and business had played a big role for decades, but now the company was considering broadening its offering after being forced to choose differently during the closed years. The private market required more and different tools, the company reasoned, but it could still be interesting if the products were better adapted and the requirements reflected in the price.

They had decided to invest in other types of support systems to enable and follow customers more closely. The internal innovations were about securing new markets, alternative target groups, reviewing the product mix, and building a CRM structure. The wind had turned and the company started producing profits, which was important for its long-term survival.

Much of customer orientation is about building relationships with the most important and carefully selected segments. We perceive that companies are increasingly empowering their departments with more open guidelines for the people involved. It's faster to initiate contacts through the various online platforms and have short introductions, while the messages are still growing in the way that people meet in real life. Several companies accept a hybrid work model after COVID-19 as an option, and for a traveling salesperson, the net could mean increasing initial contacts. We also see that more organizations are leaving the traditional structure focused on customers with research and development, marketing, sales, and service. There is more focus on behaviors, understanding pricing, and being able to use data to understand customer attributes. It is, of course, influenced by the size of the company, data maturity, and the willingness of management to work more unconventionally. Regardless, sales work needs to include focus and priorities and ensure that the new business is in line with the existing business model.

The best projects have developed and clarified a good marketing strategy, deepened the knowledge of the current business model, and gradually tried to crack the customer code. They always work proactively, follow their business more closely, and usually have a customer manager/responsible individual for the client as this ensures the relationship is grounded and that regular meetings with the customer for follow-ups and evaluations occur. It's about being able to be both businesslike and offer empathy at the same time. In the big picture, this makes it easier to negotiate customer benefit with prices that match customer expectations and be able to make active changes that contribute to a common benefit and knowledge development.

> The large industrial company with factories throughout Europe had in recent years put considerable resources into going through its current and future products. This had meant several joint international meetings on descriptions, inventory questions, issues related to purchasing and a development in the article database. The company was now thinking about changing its sales department to fit the right products.
>
> After a few months, the company decided to develop its business model with a combined indoor and outdoor sales unit. By reducing items by almost 30 percent due to old or outgoing products, inside sales could be shaped as an order unit that could respond and recommend products.
>
> The external sales unit conducted several conferences that developed more knowledge of the content of the deals and the arguments were sharpened. There were great advantages in bringing the organizations together to clarify the structures, share experiences, create a positive feeling, and put together new activity plans. New innovations were planned out, and after a customer study conducted between seminars, conditions were also created for a new product group. The overall focus was opportunities, needs, channels, and margins/costs.

In the projects, it is an advantage to see opportunities and be open to developing new and existing values. Our view is that both the existing business model and the one that is developed/improved should have value-creating activities linked at each level of management, regardless of what the organizations look like. We see that the better companies have more activity around value creation and that it contributes to new innovation projects. They follow driving forces more actively and have ongoing reconciliations with their customers.

> Over the past ten years, the company had become market leaders in its field of industry. They had a business strategy building on values and with a good positioning. The company had ongoing reconciliations, focused on a valuable solution, and actively prioritized their business model. It was about creating a profitable, safe, and developing process with a good product.
>
> The owners gave the board instructions to go forward and try to build a customer-oriented structure that could develop facts and contribute to better decisions. They suggested that the management should simplify their business model even more and take away some services that were performed with partners.

The company conducted ongoing qualitative studies for almost ten years and these served as leverage for continued knowledge development. This time they did a separate study with customers and combined it with outside experts in the field. The management team discussed the conclusions in five seminars and made changes. Some were related to the distribution of responsibilities and others were about better cash flows.

We have seen that increased focus in the early processes of value creation can contribute with more solutions and later better collaborations and profits. New products and services can emerge by remaining in the questions, deepening conversations with customers, and focusing on driving forces and connections. Our view is that good companies stimulate innovation development when they increase proximity to the customer with follow-up and by continuously highlighting good common examples. It can be about going through the projects afterward, having seminars on completed productions or letting external experts give their views on the implemented changes. The changes with innovation often come from internal or external driving forces that create new needs, which in turn enables concepts.

Insights for customer management structure

1. Work proactively with a customer manager
2. Follow early process of value creation and make an inventory
3. Build important relationships in carefully selected segments
4. Deepen knowledge of the current business model
5. Set a marketing strategy for innovation projects

Increase market knowledge, customer needs, sharpen offers, and create joint ventures and new strategies

The good medium and large companies follow national and international markets, news, and trends on a daily basis from the outside world, local markets, industries, certain selected customer groups, and their competitors. In these companies, there is often a story that is told in their ongoing annual reports and there the markets are presented as opportunities, effects on selected areas are highlighted, and limitations are scrutinized. Information has become more open, accessible, and concentrated. There is also in-depth knowledge in most areas that can also be supported with university theses. The digital medium has moved us closer to all available markets and it feels like we are on the streets of New York or on Venice Beach in Los Angeles when the cameras zoom in as we watch on our mobile phones.[5]

Today, many people listen to podcasts from all over the world, follow sporting events from different places on television or digitally, and receive more and more targeted advertising from algorithms. When we move into the digital world, we are more visible than before and possibly monitored with cameras and followed by our IP address from the mobile phone, regardless of where we are in the world.[6] The more active companies can develop smart strategies to follow their customers' events very closely, almost real time, and see how their attributes develop.

The availability of products through improved transport, techniques, and information has also changed marketing that needs to be refined and further adapted to get through to the target market. Consumers today are more agile than before and get access to news directly through more targeted channels. It could be described as the customer is moved in different stages from the outer world to gradually becoming more and more interested and finally buying that iPad and concluding by reading the instruction sheet about all the possibilities. As more decisions increase, we are also more dependent on what others think and companies secure themselves through reader groups, targeted focus groups, and quick premiums. The new services in user experience (UX) in recent years are examples of the increased user interest.[7]

> *The international company had had a fantastic development since entering into a new collaboration with a previous supplier and had been able to develop more and better products. Turnover quickly passed several hundred millions and the positive results came with it. It also provided an opportunity to distribute the different tasks to a number of different countries: strategy development, business model/business planning, product development, marketing, production, quality control, overall marketing, logistics, and administration.*
>
> *The head company was responsible for the business model, marketing, and product development. All companies within the group were responsible for their respective markets with their own administration and gradually built-up awareness through broad campaigns that quickly had an impact. Customer development focused on the value of the business model with leading products for certain given target groups.*
>
> *Major investments were made to be able to offer products before they were manufactured, produced, controlled, and shipped to the various markets with container traffic and trucks. It was crucial to be able to sell through platforms and through distributors. The company's own organization handled material, descriptions of various kinds, and supported the platforms and the network of distributors. Some managers were responsible for mapping the larger agreements and ensured business before ordering and inventory management was outsourced with invoicing afterwards.*

The good companies are active in the market and acquire knowledge before their competitors through high activity. The proactive posture generates and stimulates new insights and often completely new behaviors are involved. We have observed that good companies are more interested in the development of their products and services than others and at the same time follow their business processes with better control. Customers' current buying behavior will affect future demand, which we usually remind clients of at our introductory seminars. The company's development needs to constantly work for better customer value and constantly pay attention to the delivery capacity and the actual deliveries.

Technological development has made it possible to more easily follow and document customer benefits. The number of products available has made consumers more sensitive, volatile, and unfaithful to brands. This is especially noticeable when older and younger groups are compared; the younger customers switch faster and prefer the new media. There are almost no people under the age of 30 who have subscriptions to traditional newspapers; instead, there are groups of people over the age of 50 left in the old business model. The younger groups instead read and listen to blogs, read newspapers and articles online, and consume podcasts/apps. The challenges right now are about adding value more quickly and efficiently than their competitors, choosing the right path and commercializing faster.

When the international company opened the local company many years ago, there was a very extensive knowledge of what values were created in the world in this industrial field. The company's focus on the business model had been created over several years with qualified unique products. They had grown with their customers and continued to deliver unique solutions that were often built together on site, which later also meant that a service function was formed to provide spare parts when something broke.

The unique solutions were limiting for the international buyer, as although the price of the products was good, there was no scalability in the business model. The company had its own sales organization that prioritized outreach, displays of existing customers' solutions for potential and long closing times. The international owner gradually wanted to use his broad marketing organization and develop sales through retailers/distributors with a cheaper product that could be sold to more people.

There was a battle over which innovations created the most value and, if so, how the market organization would be redirected. The current organization had good knowledge of segments and built-up relationships and felt a great self-confidence with the existing product. The international owner wanted to scale and change the processing to reach more people. They decided to conduct a comprehensive qualitative study to prepare for a change and idea meetings with management.

One point of business innovation is to be able to use resources and collaborations differently and in more countries. We see that our customers can more easily add value with a more open approach to resource use. At the same time, it requires that companies are not afraid to change the structure of the existing business model and can see benefits in the changed process of new alternative strategies. These exercises should be able to measure quantities, be secured with financial data, and be assessed with key factors/resources.

As the world becomes one large marketplace rather than different countries with different markets, the ability to reach a global customer base becomes ever more important. By being able to allocate resources, building international delivery solutions, and assessing data that comes from literally all over the world, it means that businesses can build and maintain relevance to the customers that exist globally. Companies of any size that want to orient themselves toward the international market must be able to be outward-looking, flexible, and adaptive to whatever changes may occur from resource availability to changes in customer consumption.

> *The midsize company handled large quantities of product between customers and suppliers. They had a long-established business model with good customer knowledge and a fairly clear idea of which channels worked best. Profitability had also been on the rise for many years.*
>
> *In the past year, the CEO of the company had started talking about retirement and at the same time the management felt that some of the larger customers were not buying in the same volumes anymore. They argued that customer value had changed due to technology, allowing customers to be able to buy more easily from other competitors.*
>
> *After a comprehensive customer study, the company changed its marketing strategy by offering new value propositions to two new segments in the same industry with a positioning that was more based on quality and higher price and was less dependent on the outgoing CEO. This meant that production was divided into several units and several parts were instead produced in other countries, which led to better profitability.*

The medium and larger companies need to have continuous market contact to follow trends and driving forces, understand what skills are needed, and be able to act to ensure the necessary resources. A larger organization can distribute resources to more people and thus also reduce the risks for its larger customers.

We see that changes in existing business models are often due to the outside world as much as internal conditions when it comes to value-creating issues. It does not always have to be extensive external changes that go quickly but it can concern the changed buying behaviors of existing customer groups who have noted alternative values in their competitors during some trip to another country and now want to change their strategies. The internal drivers are often related to the loss of key employees in sales and marketing, the change of senior leaders, and changes in ownership. They can also be a combination where a material resource is missing, expired, or needs to be replaced because of its poor quality.

Insights for increasing market knowledge

1. Acquire knowledge through activity
2. Follow consumers who are volatile and unfaithful to brands
3. Establish reverse mentorship, with younger groups mentoring older groups
4. Search for trends, driving forces, and skills in other countries
5. Distribution of resources and values for reducing risks

Focus on opportunities – needs, resources, and solutions together with measurement/follow-up

Increased globalization has had several consequences in 2020 when large parts of the world were affected by COVID-19. Technological developments took the impact of the pandemic straight into homes by the spreading of globalization's effects, showing overcrowded hospitals and sharing common messages about how best to protect us from the disease. The world showed that globalization can also mean that we focus on opportunities even when the worst happens by everyone contributing to survival strategies.[8] The big difference in modern society is that access to information and communication is faster, but also that we need to understand the different cultural differences between people and countries. We can fly from Stockholm to Nice in less than three hours, a journey that previously took days and weeks.

Companies need to think bigger as business plans become more comprehensive but also with more detail about customer needs. A deeper understanding of these requirements helps the company focus on the right resources and knowledge. There are very few customers who do not appreciate an added value; in fact, quite the opposite. It requires the company to search, sort, analyze, and later evaluate how they can create world-class value.

We have tested simpler innovations several times in difference cases and then our customers have invited their client base to take the proposal further. Deeper understanding that comes out well once has a greater chance of finding the right solutions again and again. There is always a risk that customers may be provoked when companies are proactive, but when the value is there they will adapt. If the innovations have unique values, it is better to move forward than to sit still and miss opportunities that otherwise would not have arisen.

The development of customer value is about not only searching for needs but also offering the right skills that contribute to delivering the value that the agreement actually applies to. The internationalization of services and products has been helped by free trade and the flow of capital between countries. Our innovation projects have an advantage when we can seek resources more freely and switch actors or partners in the business model between several countries. We see that companies quite often acquire new assets to strengthen their models if the quantity is large enough or move operations to another country to save costs.

To overcome larger costs and cut margins, we work together in the projects to constantly find innovations that can be offered to more people at an alternative price. At this moment in time, values need to gather strength around energy and climate issues, according to large parts of the world's scientists, so that Antarctica's ice sheets are not lost, and work can be done to change the dramatic warming that is happening on Earth. Companies around the world have the task of switching to more sustainable alternatives and seeing new opportunities in alternative value creation.

> The company was concentrated around major cities with a well-thought-out business model adapted to customers and focused on their value-creating activities. They worked actively to improve their structure with their own key resources and partners. The whole orientation was to be at the forefront with their deliveries and also question their resources on an ongoing basis in everything from human, organizational, and physical factors.
>
> They had ongoing follow-up meetings every week with the customers who were the largest or had other influence, had a built-in service for complaints, and were able to report errors and staffed on-call responders together with the customers while they also had their own on-call processes as well. The company reasoned that the level of service was one of the keys to their success. In the annual follow-up surveys, most things were on top.
>
> In recent years, customers had had comments that the structure of the organization could mean that some simple decisions took too long and, above all, they were afraid of the future because the company was facing natural age changes. Against this background, they conducted a larger customer study with internal anchoring seminars. This later led to several changes in the internal structure to ensure that the delivery of the business model became even better.

When companies focus and prioritize value-creating activities, it can also mean that customers are provoked as there is change to a product or service that they have come to rely on, but that does not stop the better companies. It challenges its customers more with alternative solutions and offers support for change, which often creates added value for both. They have built-in meetings and points of contact with each other that focus on value-creating activities. These can be about highlighting good examples, going on joint study trips, reviewing production details on site, visiting alternative partners included in the deliveries, having joint seminars on topics that affect the joint business, walking around the premises/areas included in the assignment, empowering appointed people further, training each other in being proactive, and so on.

The more aggressive companies also have more thoughtful, detailed, and focused strategies that help develop the business. We see that form is not always decisive for success, but rather activity is a far better predictor. It is clear that the leader of our change projects must be able to assess how much new knowledge is needed to strengthen the model. That knowledge may be more of an estimate or an assessment from the start, but it is later an active part of our seminars after completing the study and later when we finalize an activity plan for implementation of numbers of innovation projects.

The international medium-sized company was the market leader, highly renowned, and was known for its fantastic products with wide offerings. The internal culture was about being solution-oriented, focusing on the customers, being accessible, creating sustainable relationships, and offering a collaboration beyond the ordinary.

The entire range characterized the good collaborations and the company had annual traditional user meetings that were appreciated and contributed to a family atmosphere. Despite all the superlatives, they experienced that the market was beginning to change and decided to carry out an innovation process to initially create an understanding of their business model at that moment in time.

They had some initial ideas about expanding into other areas but they also had a fear that their situation would be exposed to competition with cheaper products from other countries. The innovation project lasted almost three years with trimmed strategies and reaching several new markets with a value positioning relating to earlier successes. It led to a growth of 30 percent per year, 20 percent better margins and better profits overall.

In the projects, it is important to be able to think bigger and develop concepts that can add value without losing sight of the reality of the customer and the marketplace. When we conduct seminars after a qualitative study, whether it is internal, external, or a combination of both, the focus is initially on the study's analysis and conclusions. The ambition is to be able to identify development projects that add value to the business model through approximately two to six seminars. We encourage the groups to think big, ideally outside the box, and carry out brainstorming activities. The outcome usually generates about 20 to 40 realistic improvements for bottlenecks and/or completely new proposals. After that, we break them down into groups by coding different subject areas and priorities and finally we put names in an activity plan that the management should be able to implement moving forward. The unrealistic proposals often disappear when we test them in different scenarios and ultimately assess the economic impact of the proposals. It is about creating solutions that strengthen customer benefit, that use existing or new resources efficiently, and that are possible to follow up in concrete ways.

> *Despite the company's size of about 300 employees and operating in many locations, they set an example in their deliveries and customers were very satisfied. They had an in-depth focus on customer behavior and made continuous reconciliations on their delivered services.*
>
> *The company's communication to their customers involved ongoing interviews with key customers, recurring surveys, customer events, and other joint activities. Above all, customers appreciated the high level of service as something out of the ordinary and it justified a higher price than that of their competitors. The company focused on its image and often shared it with customers, which reinforced the feeling that it was chosen.*
>
> *The company feared an upcoming change in structure and decided to conduct a study of the existing business model in order to map the outside world and build a picture of the opportunities ahead. This led to a four-year positive journey of change. The new renovated business model included a clearer need with a value contribution that could be measured and followed up for two new segments of costumers.*

To create a deeper understanding of customer behavior and open better access to key resources, it requires a curiosity and willingness to contribute with more knowledge. Innovation projects are often based on driving forces, which help when the existing business model is to be analyzed and later when a qualitative study is to be carried out. We believe that the start of the projects need time to enable later anchoring. A good process needs to be co-creative, but this does not mean that behaviors that hinder the business should be avoided. The project can contribute with increased understanding and a connection to the causes of those hindrances and then work to correct them.

As companies grow and change their business models, it controls the structure and that requires anchoring. When we see that there is a pronounced customer need but the internal resistance exists in opposition or escalates, we usually recommend more time and conversation before the next step. It may also include contacts with trade union representatives, human resources (HR), or other experts. In a strong company, this is a positive opportunity for change. Companies that do not change risk their entire existence, and larger companies reason that change is necessary for survival.

Insights for creating opportunities

1. Generate thoughtful, detailed, and focused strategies
2. Think bigger; add value without losing sight in reality
3. Focus on customer behavior and access to key resources
4. Visualize alternative solutions and offers support for change
5. Prioritize value-creating activities

Focus on margins and deliveries

Global growth is expected to continue, and studies often speculate that volumes are roughly doubling based on current trajectories. China, India, and the United States are expected to be at the forefront of growth, which is primarily technology-driven.[9] This development is more about replacing technologies in already-existing industries, which should mean that more people are in jobs but it also indicates these will be positions with lower wages.[10] The big challenge is to increase the focus early on for total volumes and margins in the business model. Within the next ten years, technology development will continue to focus on cloud computing, virtual and augmented reality, AI, and education.[11]

Driving forces, proximity to customers, creating a market structure, choosing segments, increasing understanding of the business model's value, and focusing on the opportunities go a long way to creating strong symbiotic relationships. However, customers also buy results; they want to follow a story, get an experience, and want to perceive that their deliveries should make a difference. The whole game is about challenging convention, showing your solutions, daring to test and measure. A business model needs boldness and focus on the economic space, including margins. It can be about the margins of the products or services that remain after production or the profit margins for the whole that decrease if the company can reduce its costs. It may sound tedious to also have to prioritize costs in both the development of the model's creation and when the latter is up and working but it can show net positive results. The economic space enables continued expansion and when the value is priced to the customer, it is important that the costs of producing and delivering are included.

The second parameter is the ability to deliver the predetermined content, timing, and costs. When the trains do not follow the schedule, when flights are canceled, or the pizza delivery is wrong, we react with emotion and want a price reduction or complain about the entire delivery. If we get reasonable explanations in time and there is a built-up trust based on previous experience, we are prepared to forgive more. Companies constantly risk losing trust if they do not secure their deliveries; we are as good as our last output that creates our next input. By securing the entire process of the business model, they can deliver according to customer expectations, no more and no less. If the company over-delivers against the customer's expectation, it indirectly means worse margins, a lower price, and worse outcomes in the result statement.

A medium-sized industrial enterprise had undergone a number of changes in recent years and had begun the development of products and services for the long term. It was possible to create new projects, but gradually the management began to notice that the long-term margins largely disappeared when costs skyrocketed in the early activities. There were absolutely no errors with the business model but the initial price was not enough to bear the development in the long run.

To increase knowledge, the company purchased support and calculated each project with external help. Quite quickly, it became clear that the projects were too small and the margins would not be enough with the costs that were needed. For another company that already had volume, it would work better. The company decided to wind up the projects and build a new organization with projects that could bear the costs all the way.

The new organization would cover entire deliveries where development was the first step and management the last. They mapped, conducted interviews, had meetings, and about a year later were able to sell the projects with a smaller profit and thus had reduced the risks of future losses.

Customer value cannot be underestimated or overvalued but needs to describe a real value without uncertainty and guesswork. It is a difficult balancing act when products and services are to be developed because a lot can happen that has the potential to affect price. We have seen that external factors in particular are often the part of budgets that fail and, in several situations, could have been handled in another way from the start. We usually touch on external points in connection with the review of the existing business model: increased environmental requirements, political costs, technology, globalization (low-priced imports), trends (smaller market, industry slippage, capital availability, assortment issues, skills transfer, and more), legislation, and the world economy. It can also be about new players in the industry, new products, a changed customer need and changed buying needs. It is a complex question to predetermine prices that both need relevant facts and are ideally supplemented with experience.

It is equally important when focusing on the deliveries, which are often dependent on the entire chain. They need to be planned, managed, and delivered on time and with the right products. It is about delivering the quality that companies have agreed with their customers and at the level of service that they prefer. There are many different shipping solutions and the customer needs to be involved and have the ability to choose based on their preferences. During the pandemic, online purchases increased and thus home deliveries did as well. Most of the companies that had operations already running and could deliver to homes did so. Other companies, such as restaurants, had to develop a new solution to help them survive; at that stage, a cold burger with fries was certainly okay but now that we have the pandemic behind us it is less likely to be acceptable. Most customers are discerning and as the flow of information has increased, customers have become more mobile.

> The international company had developed administrative programs/ business systems that were used successfully in various segments. Their main segments showed worrying trends where more players would compete in the same market, an upcoming change with the redistribution of resources, and a change in consumption behavior due to new technologies.
>
> The company operated in several continental markets and the home market was considered an important mirror as Sweden was far ahead in technological development. They decided to carry out an innovation process with initial talks, a qualitative study, and then seminars to be able to get a better basis for how the existing business model possibly needed to be adapted.
>
> The innovation process confirmed the market's changes and pointed to several drivers: changing behavior, brand fidelity increasing, a central brand platform to meet the threats, focus on content, and customers felt they had to take a position to survive. For the company, this meant working with changed margins but also being more careful about how customers would cope with their transition. The company also improved its delivery reliability and then began segmentation toward a number of new markets that had been on the radar, primarily in other countries. The whole process was successful and took over three years to complete.

International companies usually have better opportunities to create new collaborations and develop other deliveries. Initial margins may be smaller to gain access to the alternative markets, but also because the large part of the development costs have already been taken care of. This is possibly because the general cost structure looks different in a new country in which the product is launched. When we conduct seminars after our studies, there are questions that often come into focus, such as can we have two different prices for different groups with approximately the same products? For the projects, margins and deliveries are part of the business model and how profitability is handled is very different from company to company if everything is about the financial space. The larger companies are better placed to act in the longer term with their built-up administrations, productions, marketing and sales organizations, and the availability of capital. Critics would certainly argue that they do not have the flexibility and therefore rather get to devote themselves to developing existing products and services.

> *The international manufacturer was clearly market-dominant in its field, offering a full-service concept and gradually adding alternative possibilities to prices. The market had changed and several of their past most important retailers/stores were having a tough time, especially as the manufacturer's prices had been raised and the stores had lost customers to their competitors.*
>
> *Their market situation was good, but if 30 percent of the market were to disappear, there would be a major impact on those factories. To create better data/facts, the company decided to carry out an innovation project with existing customers, potential customers, other experts, and its own sales organization.*
>
> *The aim was to secure existing margins and increase growth. The interviews confirmed the risk by identifying the upcoming driving forces to come. In the seminars that followed after the studies, the management created two new products to meet the change by offering a new financial product. The project was successfully implemented over 18 months.*

Work with margins is linked to the price that customers are prepared to pay and for companies it is about deepening knowledge of the conditions that apply to the customer to be able to crack the code. Revenue is an important part of the whole, but it can also be difficult during a change process to clarify an exact new price. We always have an ambition to contribute to how the company can work with the process, and in most projects, we have been able to set overall goals and deliver detailed projects with clear margins for improvement. The strong companies usually have a desire to improve and develop their business models together with their customers. They work more with open processes, straightforward communication, and focus on world-class deliveries.

Insights for margins and deliveries

1. Describe real customer value without uncertainty.
2. Explain the agreed margins that the customer is prepared to pay.
3. Predetermine prices with facts and experience.

4. Open processes, communication, and world-class deliveries.
5. Focus on deliveries from start to finish.

Summary

Putting a company's customers at a focal point is a great way to help keep a changing market firmly in sight. When an organization spends too much time looking inward and focusing on internal processes and procedures, it can lead to losing touch with what the customer is looking for and how best to deliver the products and services. When moving toward strengthening, it is critical to have an international outlook to be able to change faster. Part of this outlook includes taking the time to do an inventory of external driving forces and having an interest in different customer groups, which will include an inventory of the product that is currently ready for customer distribution. In doing so, time will not be wasted in creating something that already exists, which in turn will give time and energy toward identifying future valuable needs the customer may have and allow for efficient customer management. The final piece of the puzzle when strengthening the focus on the customer is to identify and develop new values over putting energy into existing values. If the customer is currently satisfied with how a company is operating, take the time to project forward, look toward future trends and customer needs so that when change comes the company is best positioned to react quickly and effectively.

Management structure can also go a long way toward putting the customer at the core of a business. In mid-to-large-sized companies, having a dedicated customer manager to be responsible for following customer businesses will ensure that the relationship with customers domestically and internationally will be proactive and robust. It is often far too easy to let the day-to-day working processes to take up management's attention, which in turn leads to neglecting the very people and organizations that make business possible. The early processes of value creation can contribute with more solutions, which in turn will create stronger collaboration and better profits in the future. The real key to customer orientation is in building relationships, but particularly with the most important and carefully selected segments; where the market leader goes, other businesses and industries will follow. Having a clarified and strong marketing strategy always includes a deepened knowledge of the current business model, with more activity around value creation that contributes to new innovation projects. It may seem obvious, but in some respects going back to basics with management in clarifying the importance of developing customer-focused strategies cannot be underestimated.

When embarking on change projects, it is not enough to take the time to get a sense of where the customer base is and what it's doing today; a business that will have greatest chance of success in evolving will be active in the market and continuously acquire knowledge before their competitors so that they can constantly work for better customer value. The modern world has allowed for a wider variety of products to be on the market at any given time so that contemporary consumers are more sensitive, volatile, and less likely to be faithful to brands if they can find better value in a similar product elsewhere.

It can also be forgotten how a company evolves – when bursting onto the scene a new company is the hottest thing going, with exciting new products and services that capture attention, particularly of the younger members of the workforce. However, as a company ages, they must keep their eyes on what the new generations of managers, leaders, and thinkers need and how they take up new information. By keeping a focus on where people are looking for the newest information, a company can put itself forward in the formats that will keep them in the sights of the new market share that enters the workforce; rather than publishing books and magazine articles alone, a business can target online media, apps, and podcasts to capture attention.

A company that is knowledgeable can use its resources and collaborations differently in more countries, which means they can follow trends and driving forces while understanding the skills needs in each region. In this way, an organization can distribute its resources and values to more people and thus also reduce the risks for its larger customers domestically and internationally. Knowledge cannot be concrete. It must constantly be nurtured and grown, both within a business and how they share their products and services with the outside world. The minute that a company says, "We are the business and market leaders, we know everything we need to know," that business begins its slide into obscurity and irrelevance.

Part of the joy of a company that is willing to undertake a process of change is that it is a chance to take a look at opportunities that might not have been considered in the past. It is a time to be more thoughtful and to generate detailed and focused strategies that help develop the business. It is a time to be able to think bigger and to develop habits that can add value without losing sight of the reality of the customer and market. Deeper understanding of customer behavior and better access to key resources requires a curiosity and willingness to contribute with more knowledge. Something that can be scary but have massive positive effects is to challenge customers in new ways with alternative solutions that include offers of support of the change. When companies focus on and prioritize value-creating activities, it can also mean that customers are provoked to be more active in the business relationship.

Customer value cannot be underestimated or overvalued but needs to describe a real value without uncertainty or guesswork. It is essential to have a clear picture so that the margins the customer is prepared to pay match the quality that the companies have agreed to with their customers and that they have the level of service that is expected of their client base. It is a complex issue to predetermine prices that need relevant facts and that are supplemented with experience, and so having open processes, straightforward communication, and focus on world-class deliveries goes a long way toward customer satisfaction and willingness to carry on in a relationship. However, it is not enough to simply have agreements and work contracts in place – it is crucial to deliver as expected, which is often dependent on the entire chain. Therefore, talking the talk must be backed up by walking the walk.

Customers are the lifeblood that keeps the business going. Without people investing in what is being produced, a company quickly becomes only as good as its last sale. However, by orienting the focus of the business toward the customer and welcoming them to participate with the business, it will allow for greater change and dynamic results. It is something so simple but powerful enough to completely change the trajectory for the future.

Notes

1 Peter Vanham, "A Brief History of Globalization," Geo Economics, World Economic Forum, January 17, 2019, https://www.weforum.org/agenda/2019/01/how-globalization-4-0-fits-into-the-history-of-globalization/.
2 Kevin Webb, "From the Internet to the iPhone, Here Are the 20 Most Important Inventions of the Last 30 Years," *Insider*, May 17, 2019, https://www.businessinsider.com/most-important-inventions-of-last-30-years-internet-iphone-netflix-facebook-google-2019-5?op=1&r=US&IR=T.
3 Tom Petersson, *History of Swedish Business 1864–2014, del IV: 1965–1985* (Stockholm: Dialogos Förlag, 2014).
4 Marcy Farrell, "Data and Intuition: Good Decisions Need Both," Harvard Business Publishing Corporate Learning, January 6, 2023, https://www.harvardbusiness.org/data-and-intuition-good-decisions-need-both/.
5 Webb, "From the Internet to the iPhone, Here Are the 20 Most Important Inventions of the Last 30 Years."
6 Ibid.
7 Jakob Nielsen, "A 100-Year View of User Experience," NN/g Nielsen Norman Group, December 24, 2017, https://www.nngroup.com/articles/100-years-ux/.
8 Ludovic Jeanne, Sébastien Bourdin, Fabien Nadou, and Gabriel Noiret, "Economic Globalization and the COVID-19 Pandemic: Global Spread and Inequalities," *GeoJournal* 88 (2023): 1181–88.
9 Vanham, "A Brief History of Globalization."
10 Ibid.
11 Johnny Wood, "The Number of Global Patent Applications Is Breaking Records: Where Are the Hotspots?" Forum Agenda, World Economic Forum, December 19, 2022, https://www.weforum.org/agenda/2022/12/innovation-patent-filings-intellectual-property-ip-applications/.

Chapter 5

Management

The fourth theme to consider and constantly look at throughout the entire process of change in a business is management and how they operate within an organization. The various levels of leadership and the roles that they play, along with the history and legacy of a company, are all pieces to be considered and controlled to help ensure the success of a business innovation project.

Anchor the transition to the new situation

Medium and large enterprises have been able to use technological developments over the past 30 years to direct and manage outcomes regionally and internationally with the evolution of the Internet, caller ID, e-mail and text messaging, mobile broadband, iPhone, and other communication innovations.[1] The companies have encountered many external driving forces in the outside world and different perspectives from everything from the economic and financial landscape to social, technological, and cultural aspects. The leaders have navigated between all these points much like in a sailing competition on the high seas where the best boats can face the different wind conditions with the most highly trained and experienced crew. The fantastic technological developments in transport and information have also enabled the multinational companies to establish more business opportunities in different places around the world. The big advantage has been new potential segments and alternative revenue streams from other customer groups.

Global developments have radically changed the conditions for top management and how CEOs of a group are expected to control a business. Previously, a large company had a large number of staff that helped the top group management to research facts, build up decision support, communicate and inform, manage financial flows, handle administration, including IT and many more features of a business. The staffs were the management's seconded agents and handled the daily contacts and overall reporting. As

DOI: 10.4324/9781003402121-5

the larger companies have been computerized, the staffs have changed and much of the fact-finding takes place via business systems and several of the overall results or other meetings can be communicated via Microsoft Teams or some other platform. There is a risk that management and leaders who work with digital work tools may fall behind on industry knowledge as the pace of industry becomes faster and faster, so they must continuously check their assumptions in this age and ensure more than before that the decisions are based on the latest data and evidence.[2] There are almost as many different business systems worldwide as there are airlines, although a smaller number of them dominate the market.

There should be a mission that is anchored at all stages from owners, the board, and senior management. An uncertain owner can create major problems and make it impossible for the board and management to implement change. It requires an anchored mission in all three ranks, a consensus with clear goals and be capable of managing and limiting conflicts. A business model innovation project is a knowledge journey led by management; they are responsible for changing the company's strategic identity. It involves a systematic review of various activities that include thinking, planning, action, and, in the final phase, implementation. The management team needs to be given time to analyze what is divisible (scalable) and not divisible in all the issues involved. A change in the existing business model can be seen as a large boat that includes containers of knowledge and experience to be transported on an open sea where there may be no wind but there is also the potential for a storm to blow up, and despite that, the boat should have a load plan, direction of travel, final destination, and a delivery on schedule.

The company had about 60 employees in five businesses focused on service and nursing. It was run by two equal owners who were both active in the company, which meant that the board and management were not completely autonomous. To increase clarity, they had developed an advisory directive to facilitate board work and several internal management steering documents.

Despite the well-thought-out structure, there were questions that were sometimes handled at the wrong levels and therefore they decided to work with external support for the board as well as the strategic direction. The company was successful but felt that the strategies and the existing business model needed to be further improved.

They started an innovation project that was built up with different groups from each business, combined with interviews and later five strategic seminars. When the projects were completed, they were worked together into one and all employees had to participate in two seminars to give their reactions. It was focused on anchoring and getting suggestions for possible improvements and the other to celebrate a new strategy together.

We know the most successful projects have spent more time on the reasons for the needs that exist, spent more time clarifying the purpose, and initially anchor at the necessary levels. We have had entire projects that require anchoring from owners, the board, and management, but also projects that relate to a department or a product. In the latter cases, it is the authorization of the companies that determines how a project is to be anchored. It is important that management anchors the projects before the process of change begins and that there is clarity in what the project intends and has for purpose.

New managers may find it easier to search for background facts, create the initial plans but may instead lack the necessary insights or judgment required to interpret the culture and understand the decision-making processes. We sense that new managers today are expected to have greater insight and knowledge already at hand when they start than in the past, but there are always legacies from previous leaders that are difficult to interpret outside a company. In slightly larger companies, there are people who have the knowledge and can help with the interpretations later. Most companies have the legacy of old leaders and better companies handle knowledge more openly.

There are great gains in customer management if companies can identify future valuable needs that can be transformed faster than others with a good business model. We know that medium-sized companies often end up with issues that are more about internal obstacles and the organization than creating new business. This also applies to larger companies, but it is mainly a culture of legacy that usually puts an end to changes. Older leaders are more experienced and often wise but can also have very concrete views on the way things ought to be done and what a successful outcome "should" look like. Younger managers have a more open approach to being a manager and share more of the skills that build new knowledge. It feels hopeful for the future and, above all, for continued knowledge development.

The company was a subsidiary of a large international industrial group. They had a unique knowledge within the group and the management was new at the same time that the existing business solution needed to be clarified. The company had over 90 percent of its revenue internally distributed worldwide. There was a great upside to external customers but also an anchoring process at many levels.

They assumed that it was the management that would lead the company's business and needed to go through these together without the branches of business guarding their areas, so an open climate was needed.

They started an innovation project with a two-day conference. On day one, they addressed the following: (1) What is the company's task? (2) In what areas should we operate? (3) What areas should we have? (4) How do we allocate our common resources? On day two, they painted a vision for points one through four then focused on: (5) How should we work to achieve that goal picture? (6) Which strategies, organization, and business models should be adapted? (7) Set the goal is to produce material for the next conference in about one month. The initial work led to extensive positive changes in knowledge development and sales and contributed to improvements throughout the group.

Most organizations have legacy from old leaders and the better companies try to reduce the restrictive impact by opening the processes. When we conduct the first seminars after the study, the ambition is to create an open and inclusive approach where everyone should be able to be present and get to know each other's different problems that may exist. It is about training the groups to identify, rank, and prioritize their opportunities and problems. The various seminars are conducted, with two to six of them one to two weeks apart, and after a few months, there is a plan that everyone in the management has been involved in creating.

The large worldwide company developed and integrated systems and was one of the leading companies in its niche. The political developments of recent years had benefited their business model and more decisions were expected to come in the coming years.

The management and the company as a whole felt a tailwind but at the same time were questioning whether they would be able to cope with the expected volume with current resources and needed to think, plan, and probably implement some change.

They started an innovation project together with the management in two seminars where the purpose was to map the existing business with a focus on structure and key resources with two focus groups. In the first seminar, it emerged that there were probably resources for the picture painted by the groups. They were all given tasks with a number of internal interviews between the two seminars (about four weeks since this was a half-day management meeting that was extended to a full day), and at the second meeting the picture was confirmed, which could later be anchored.

A business model innovation process is simplified if the CEO is included in the decision-making chain from the start to be able to anchor with the board and owners if necessary. It is a prerequisite that the anchoring is carried out so that the company can develop a more profitable process and not end up at unnecessary dead ends later on in a change process.

The best companies work on leading through others and understanding is an important incentive for behavioral changes that the company should also implement. In its implementation, the company relies on the various considerations being made, and success is about the new strategies being transformed into actions. If not all the pieces of the puzzle are put together or there is a lack understanding of any party that is involved, then it will be difficult to implement. An implementation can therefore be described as sailing in a tailwind, various crosswinds, and sometimes in full headwinds. The boat should have a clear direction of travel and be able to sail in good wind conditions with a sea-accustomed crew.

Insights for anchoring the transition to the new situation

1. Control of manager's insight and knowledge from start
2. Include the CEO in the decision-making process in the project
3. Handle past legacy from leaders in a more open way
4. Focus on future valuable needs
5. Secure the purpose and intent of the project with anchoring

Clarify strategies and business solutions – create broader knowledge about business information

Technological development has made it easier to get an overview of a business model, but it can still be challenging with many parts that are included in products being produced in many places around the world. Management should be able to have an overview of a business model and identify driving forces that need to be managed step by step by using technological equipment to relate to and understand the data.[3] When it needs to change, the leader has to admit that more information is needed, not accuse others, particularly if it has come as a surprise, so that they can sum up the issues and then clarify the path forward. The initial information gathering can be handled with specific examples that have open-ended questions. The next step is to go on to explain why it is needed through repetition and become more and more specific. Medium and large companies are complex things that include individuals with many lived experiences and are often based on stories that are an important part of the soul of the company. What distinguishes good companies from those that perform more poorly is that they have a more active signal system linked to the driving forces with a more active leadership.[4]

As data develop, we have noticed that management and leadership are more divided than before. In the past, the manager acted more through their internal staff and perhaps controlled more through country managers or the subsidiaries through active reporting. Today, communication is more widespread and faster, which requires the management to stand behind the decisions more openly and harmonize messages and behaviors, and to foster the ethos that performance grows through loyalty.[5] It contributes to a better result by making successive changes to the existing business model faster. Management has the ultimate responsibility for ensuring the strategic direction that will support and develop the business in the best way.

For the top echelon management, it is difficult to create a business model that can avoid bottlenecks with a clear value position and strong robust strategies. They need to be clear about values, interested in behaviors, preferably be both creative and logical and constantly work to ensure that the company works to improve its own values. Management needs to run their businesses like they are driving a train successfully from London to Paris with customers who paid a price according to their expectations, get service on board in comfortable seats, can charge and use all their electronic devices in the carriage, be able to choose to sit in a carriage that is quiet or allows calls, and last, but most importantly, arrives at the agreed time. They must lead by example, whether it is the ordinary course of business or if there are ongoing business model innovation projects. We see a trend that many CEOs have become younger when they take office but stay for shorter periods of time than before in their roles. In contrast, the average age of board directors is usually over 60 or older in larger multinational corporations.

The midsize group had grown to be close to 200 employees and were now one of the major players in the region with a focus on personal service. There were also more companies within the group that could collaborate and add value.

The business environment was clear; they were all over the region, had developed good relationships with their customers, had delivered well in all channels, and had good quality ratings. The owner wanted to develop his management more to be able to move on, but several of the employees had worked for too short a time to step into a more senior role.

The company decided to carry out an innovation project to create a clearer strategy for the business model and also review the bottlenecks that existed in production. They initiated business meetings, conducted an internal study, and held conversations in general. This led to the management being expanded with a Vice President who had experience in the field and was able to take over the management of the staff as the company was staff-intensive.

It is important that management stands behind the decisions and harmonizes messages and behaviors. The strategies need to be clear and help management to lead the business model. The most important behaviors should be thought through and planned to facilitate future work with the innovation project. It will include what the framework should look like for the project, allocated budget, times, meetings, follow-up, and deliverables.

It requires management to lead by example and understand that the project may need time for understanding and that they must act with care. We have experienced that after the initial conversations, the CEO sometimes starts changes on their own and also started parallel studies when we conducted studies. This can be a problem in that it can make it difficult to determine the state of things in the business if the state of the business continues to shift. We work with our customers' needs and show the way and how it can be done, and in this it often happens that identified bottlenecks can be addressed immediately. However, that is if it is clearly part of the existing business model, otherwise there is a risk that confidence in the project will shrink even before it has started.

> *The midsize private school company had two equal owners who knew each other well for a long time and had worked together in a public school before. The business model would create value through creativity and the school would especially invest in different creative methods. The schools were located in two middle-class areas in Stockholm with good access to customers.*
>
> *They had done external studies that showed even greater potential. The owners had appointed external expertise to the board and a few more people to the management, and one of the owners was the CEO. To increase clarity, they decided to go through their existing business model, do a study and use seminars as an idea bank for what was possible to implement.*
>
> *The owners influenced more than they understood at the start, but the project then led to a very clear creative direction that later led to success for the school. The project gained a lot from the fact that the questions were given time and that the priority was directed toward everyone being on board, understanding what needed to be done and knowledge was in focus as the creative direction needed a clear structure.*

In most projects that have major changes, there is resistance from either employees leaving the company or those struggling to stay in their roles. Our opinion is that management needs to help with understanding where the dissatisfaction lies and identify bottlenecks and behaviors that can stop the boat from turning in the wrong direction and get it back on track more actively if it strays from its course. We also see in our seminars that increased contact with customers can create faster input on what needs have not been met, which also relieves and solves problems.

> *The large industrial company had a long history in the local mill community. It had been bought by a major foreign industrial group a few years*

before and two out of three previous owners left almost immediately, but the third owner was still active in the management. The company had one CEO and a total of five people in management; it was a reasonably large business in production and was also responsible for sales in the Nordic countries.

There were some concerns that production could be moved to Southern Europe due to a better cost structure, but the company still had enough specialists that this could not happen. They decided to start one-to-one meetings to finance the business and explain the business model.

What spoke in favor of a move was that the tools for creating the unique products were expensive and the new owner would probably prioritize moving the business if the investments became too large. After a year of support, the company conducted a study and from a number of seminars later it became clear that the main part of the production would be moved while a sales office would remain there.

We know that increased awareness of the business model can create creativity and better values. Those values include a clearer structure, the right skills of the key employees, a good model for empowerment, a program for knowledge development, and more persistent knowledge. Our view is that performance also grows through employee loyalty when there is a willingness to deliver in harmony with the company's values and long-term goals. For management, it is crucial to gain access to employees' energy to create better outcomes from the projects. One part of what we are working on is to make each step-by-step part of improving a business model visible and focus toward a profitable process. By having success factors as a mirror when the development seminars are conducted, management can focus more on the content and future actions in the form of an action plan.

Insights for clarifying the business model

1. Stand behind decisions, messages, and behaviors
2. Lead by example with time and acting with care
3. Identify bottlenecks and behaviors
4. Increase creativity and better values
5. Use success factors as a mirror for possible implementations

Form an open, present, and courageous solution – capture heritage and look at opportunities

Digital technology has changed the conditions for collecting, analyzing, and developing data for medium and large companies. The new electronic methods with the Internet have allowed people to inform themselves today in ways that were previously unavailable. Communication has also been simplified and offers more options with e-mail, smartphones, Microsoft Teams, and other platforms. The entire leadership has had to be directed toward becoming more open, accessible, and available so that it can be understood faster in the increasingly uncertain reality faced by today's leaders.[6] Today, companies' information is more accessible than before with websites, annual reports online, and newsletters, and in many circumstances, it is possible to communicate and ask questions via a web-based chat service. We see that when new leadership is formed the digital assets are more active and bolder in its technical decisions and makes decisions based on both intuition and data.[7]

A more open solution of information and communication has a positive impact on business models. It increases opportunities for clarification and reduces the risks of missteps, misconceptions, or delivery mistakes. An open approach also gives management a stronger sense of a freer approach that also strengthens the self-esteem of the employees, leadership, and the company overall. It requires management to dare more than it has previously and allows creativity and a greater openness from how the content models are actually structured to how they work and what key factors dominate.

Accessibility to the company's customers, employees, partners, and other experts also needs to increase, but it will take longer. We have noticed that the younger leaders sometimes find it difficult to communicate this openness with their older colleagues precisely because the older view of competition is that the company's strategies are largely closed to everyone other than those who actually need to know them, particularly the leaders. An exciting alternative can then be to offer resources from outside technology experts, which provides opportunities for interaction between these experts and management who can then communicate the need for this openness to all employees and bring everyone into a shared vision moving forward.

About ten years ago, companies started offering open-plan offices and after a few years with COVID-19, it has become popular to use a hybrid working model, being able to work from home or from the office on alternate days. Prior to the pandemic, there were already moves being made for people to work in more individual ways. For example, in the office, people listen to music in earbuds instead of having a radio on and sending out sound to the entire office. For management, it is a living question how individuals, groups, and entire companies can perform in joint projects. There are different opinions about what a hybrid solution adds and loses; one issue that has been touched upon in discussion is that less time together reduces the proximity of calls and the companies' important conversations. Opponents say that it is certainly possible to keep the achievements alive via the platforms that offer live transmission.

For the innovation projects, it is an advantage if the solutions can be more permissive, more present, and with more straightforward communication. It also makes it easier if management can help empower their team to speed up and facilitate decisions. An interesting observation is that the best change projects usually have both individual and shared decision-making; some decisions are centralized and others are completely decentralized. For thinking and planning, it can be good to let more people in, but when it comes to action and implementation of the business model innovation case, more power is needed to perform.

> *The large international company was about to be bought out of the stock exchange and several of their partner organizations were owned through the company while others were privately owned. When the buyout was complete, the largest privately owned company wanted to sell its company because there was now a new platform for a buyer.*
>
> *The owner of the largest company was older and did not want to make a new investment out of motivation again and felt that the new owner group did not really give the same positive feedback. They got a long partnership agreement and were thus able to start a change.*
>
> *The company began by developing its existing business model, created a new management team, hired a consultant with knowledge of business models, and began planning to leave the business. After reviewing the state of affairs, two studies and seven seminars were made. The whole change stayed on the rails and three years later the company had new owners and two satisfied parties.*

To create an open environment, management must give confidence in creativity, proximity, and dare to be brave. Our experience is that it has been easier for the companies that are age-mixed and have equal numbers of different age groups. Of course, it becomes a generalization because there may be age-mixed groups who enjoy working in a hybrid model while others just prefer being in the office. These issues are neither black nor white; on the contrary, it depends on what management thinks for that particular company and perhaps with some reference to the various labor/work environment legislation in each individual country or jurisdiction.

In order for management to change, they need to be brave and question internal and external resistance gradually and offer some other alternative. In this, it is important to understand what are the inherited behaviors and what are potentially new behaviors brought about by the change process. We know that the open solution gives management a sense of freer approach and can therefore strengthen self-esteem because the model is perceived much more freely by management and employees. However, our view is that the majority of management in larger medium and large companies still prefer traditional forms of organization as some of their culture is about power and some is about traditions. It will take time to find a way to fold this more open approach into this traditional way of working so that they can exist together – a work environment that encourages inclusion and input from various levels while honoring the legacy of the company and allowing management to take the decisions that are necessary.

> *The large company was divided into regions and had wondered for a long time if they really offered their customers the best business model and what they could do to change the value and their offer. The question had been touched on at owners' meetings, several board meetings, and also been relevant on several occasions in the management teams of different regions.*
>
> *The company decided to conduct a qualitative study with customers in one region and a special area was selected. An innovation case was outlined in two initial meetings and then an extensive qualitative study was conducted. The results of the study were presented to the regional management who decided that focus groups should be carried out together with the most important employees, the involved customers, and a few selected experts.*
>
> *At the seminars, the participants were divided into three groups with different focuses, which were then alternated. Within nine weeks, three seminars were held, and on each occasion the results were further clarified. Since the start, the basis was a change in the direction of the business model with a number of added values, sales, and profits followed with positive results.*

When a project is to be carried out, it is advantageous if management offers an openness around materials, access to employees, customers, partners, and identifies experts. We see that there is an advantage in going through the existing model and identifying outdated routines and behaviors that may need to be changed. On several occasions we have also offered reverse mentors (younger people who can mentor some of their older colleagues) at our traditional seminars or specialized focus groups. It is mainly in the technical areas that the younger generation has more updated knowledge and the older workers can develop new knowledge faster. We also see that younger mentors have a more flexible way of working and are more naturally inclusive.

When initial reviews are made of existing business models, they also need to be validated and ensured in the decision-making forums that exist in the company. This ensures that the changes can be made visible in several stages as in most cases they also include behavioral changes that often affect existing roles of managers, groups, and employees. In our experience, the simpler changes can be decentralized almost immediately, particularly with a visibly identified bottleneck with a minor correction, while slightly larger changes need to be formalized, discussed, and later decided in the right decision forum. Our role is to help management identify issues, analyze, interpret, draw conclusions, and, where appropriate, create an offer to address how issues can be handled.

The big challenge for the medium-sized company was when the change in business model was completed, it was necessary to form a computer system that offered analysis services instead of having about a hundred employees who would perform the same task. This meant that the company would get rid of several hundred employees.

Many of these employees could be offered places with the customers who would order the services, but others had to aim for other areas of analysis. In order to speed up the knowledge acquisition, two initiating conferences, a series of interviews, and a number of subsequent seminars were conducted.

Several of the older employees chose to retire early, others decided to seek out customers, and some chose to go to other industries. It all resulted in good departures, a new range of courses from the system and several other courses that customers requested during the long process of four years.

Companies normally follow-up the implemented changes, and that is what we are trained to do. We have noticed that it is not as obvious to measure when there are major changes that affect alternative behaviors. Certainly it is possible to assess how many people were affected by the transition and how many remained or got new jobs directly within a given time interval afterward. However, behind the numbers, there are emotions, and when we use figures on an ongoing basis, we become more critical, we become corporate critics and then the assessment always goes down to the experts. Having a focus on the human element ensures that managers can be prepared to navigate numbers and changes in an open and inclusive way.

Our ambition is that there should be economic assessments to motivate and ensure the innovation processes and be able to meet the expectations that exist. It can sometimes be complicated to discern reasoning about what affects what, but usually it goes painlessly if the issues are handled openly, in a present way and with a courageous management.

Insights for capturing heritage and seeking new solutions

1. Work for an open solution with freer approach
2. Offer extended openness for fact to create better decisions
3. Offer technology mentors to speed up new knowledge acquisition
4. Give confidence in creativity, proximity, and be brave
5. Identify what can be decentralized and centralized

Lay a plan to lead through others

Today's business models are constantly exposed to influences and drivers that can be both favorable and threatening. There are constant questions about survival, especially with today's additional focus on climate and sustainability. Companies' brands are quickly affected if they do not react and act according to what customers and people actually prioritize. These are still issues that look very different around the world, but as internationalization accelerates, common purposes, policies, and later also layers of what issues are applicable are harmonized. The innovative company offers a more open, flexible, and transparent organization. For companies, it is important to have leaders who create security and go the right way in a maze of issues.[8]

In today's technological landscape, we are influenced by the leadership of others by how they think, organize, and influence their mentees to change and achieve success. Leadership is about leading others in a process, most often called social process, to carry out joint activities. Good leaders dare to challenge themselves and others and even interrogate their losses. Clear leadership is needed to succeed better with business model innovation, primarily how tasks are shared, how open communication is, and what accessibility looks like. It is about getting the change moving and how fast the leader can build their organization to get through what needs to change and then drive the model and the organization forward. A process always has behavioral issues and this will put pressure on the existing processes. The leader can be both formal and informal, while being a manager is usually a formal position.

Leading through others is seeing the company's visions and ideas come true in a chain of events. For innovation projects, it requires additional clarity as to what the project actually intends and that the leaders are prepared to participate in shaping a purpose that holds for a larger project. When the project is then underway, the leaders at different levels need to listen and be involved in what is happening regardless of what role they have in thoughts, analyses, planning, or later in an implementation. They will be role models that others can and will identify with.[9]

Since its inception 25 years ago, the company had acquired more than 200 customers on five continents and continued to develop programs and IT services successfully. The segmentation and customer groups had created lifelong relationships, and at present, they were a strong supplier in their field.

Their offer was a standard system with different modules, programming, and different types of consulting support. The unique solution created customers all over the world. At the same time, there was a need for renewal and the company had participated several times in trade fairs and gradually developed its business.

They had been negotiating with various companies to find new economies of scale but at that point they were investigating the possibility of selling part of the business. The two options did not prevent the company from looking ahead and looking for new areas, but there were questions about their segmentation that might disappear into other areas.

At the beginning of a business model innovation project, it is important that the leader(s) listen and are involved in clarifying the purpose of the project. The initial talks serve as a support for the next stage of the initial review of the business model. We have noticed that it works most painlessly when management performs a seminar, and with this as a basis, they can decide to analyze more or proceed with a study. This is so as not to put unnecessary pressure on all functions and interfere with ongoing processes. This is part of starting the processes needed for the upcoming project.

Leaders need to be able to listen and lead the way through deeper understanding and confirmation by not following all the reactions that come up from the different levels of leaders and workers. An innovation process often arouses many emotions later and there the management needs to be clear about where the company's boundaries are and how the project relates to the ongoing business. It is about clarifying boundaries at each level of the leaders and contributing to the right decisions. In being able to manage and communicate the reasoning for creating change, it will often negate any negative emotional responses and help to bring leadership around more quickly. Having grounded logic and the ability to communicate it in a meaningful way has the ability to move a change project forward while also limiting and removing obstacles that come up along the way.

The international full-service provider had spent the past five years actively working to change the business model and developed clear strategies that had served as good governance. Sales had increased by 150 percent at the same time as their previous segment underwent a major transformation and changed to a new and partly different customer area.

Through smart solutions that also included basic financing, the profit in the transition had increased by 250 percent and was now over 5 percent mirrored against the entire gross turnover. At the same time, there were concerns that the upcoming deal would be even more segmented, which risked their full-service solution as it would not work optimally.

The company needed to understand the industry logic better and decided to start an innovation project focused on the business model and with future studies and work with the company's sales organizations, both the inside and outside sales. The hope was that the studies would create new arguments and concepts that could help the industry in a transition.

In working with different cases, we are determined that leaders can act freely when setting up the project. We have noticed that in several cases the companies have a clear idea of the demarcation in tasks between the different levels that should be included in the change, but it has later been shown that it has found both inheritance from previous tasks, which had been outsourced to others, and that the leader did not have control over which tasks were carried out. There is a clear risk that the project will be limited by how management chooses and involves its team. We see that our seminars can help identify not only boundaries and roles for the coming management structure and implementation but also that these issues often affect entire companies directly. Many customers have had roles and defined job descriptions as extra seminars during ongoing projects to make the leaders in the different levels work better. Sometimes it is also one of the proposals that is included in an upcoming improvement. In several of the best processes, the companies have had the opportunity to later strengthen their general management structure in several stages because it did not exist or needed to be developed more clearly to be able to lead through others.

The large family business developed its services gradually and in recent years had pivoted to a full-service solution from development to management. The leadership had been supplemented with an external CEO to enable necessary improvements as the family increased their control as they jointly brought in structure, control, and follow-up.

When the work started, most of the work was performed through manual processes and a few years later it had progressed considerably. There were still major challenges in the various services, but the focus was mainly on the central process where the capital rate was greatest.

They built up a project organization with a project manager, an administrator, and a supervisor in place. This group was then supported by various centralized services that could help pricing, control the quality of the projects, and lead follow-up work afterward. To further strengthen the processes, an HR manager was hired and the administration was improved with various data support. They carried out several successful innovation processes that were reconciled with ongoing focus and twice a year with target seminars.

The projects need help from the leadership who can help to get their groups to think about issues, which are identified, and the attitude of the employees. It is crucial that the different levels of management receive support from the top down to managers two or three levels further down a chain. It can also apply to the entire value chain if an overall consensus is in the model. When we start new business innovation programs, we focus a lot on opportunities, improved margins, leadership, and reducing risks along the way throughout the process. Therefore, the entire management structure also needs to be updated in the business model, and if it involves a larger project, it is critical that, above all, the overall messages are handled equally in the internal and external communications.

We usually leave experiences and guiding with examples at the first meetings noting how leaders in our previous business innovation designs have acted and what challenges await to lead through others: (1) everyone work for consensus, opportunities, be good role models, simplify, find hidden resources and create more time leaders with different roles in the model; (2) the leading person should have a visionary role; (3) the next level work with boundaries and ensure resources; and (4) find ambassadors to promote the project. A major business model innovation program can last from two to five years and then the chances of succeeding with behavioral changes increase if the management gives themselves the right conditions by being empathetic role models to everyone on the team and throughout the company.

Insights for leading through others

1. Clarify the purpose of the project
2. Use seminars to analyze more and implement the project
3. Listen and lead the way through deeper understanding
4. Generate an inventory of important attributes through leadership team
5. Have different levels of management secure support

Three-Step Management

Technological development has moved humans closer together with the availability of audio files and images, regardless of whether we live in a hut, a houseboat, an apartment, a villa, or a castle. The proximity that is created through electronic media is amazing but in many ways it is also incomprehensible, as the world has become more and less predictable at once.[10] What we already know with time and space has been replaced by a flow of opportunities to travel in time around the world and get constant updates from our smartphones. The increased number of people on earth also requires continued growth, especially if technological innovations are to continue to create a better economy and quality of life going forward.

In medium and large companies, there are almost always well-thought-out structures for management and clear role descriptions that contain detailed writings about job descriptions, responsibilities, and powers (organizing, planning, and controlling). When the leaders belong to a C-suite or top management position, the contracts are often expanded with various benefits and profit-affecting variable parts, and here the contracts instead become negotiable with a salary space, including the pension. There are general rules of thumb for company type, and salaries are very different between countries because everyone must also pay tax on their salary. These management-level workers are mainly those who are involved in shaping the business model innovation projects that sometimes relate to the entire company's business model, a unit, a company in the group, or a department. They have an advantage in that they know the company's vision going forward but also a disadvantage that many of them are far from internal issues and bottlenecks.

A 1989 study showed that awareness of the problems could be 100 percent on the floor and then lose knowledge in distribution through management and that executive management knew only four percent of all problems and most of this was reporting. An important question is whether the leaders of future large companies should know more at the outset or whether they should look more at facts from data and make their own interpretations from it.[11] The successful and best business model innovation project with us has been scaled in what we call the Three-Step Management model. It is assumed that the programs are led through others at three different levels that have different stated responsibilities, which are identified and distributed in our seminars. It has been mapped better at the start, which helps management work better later when the projects become more extensive.

The international company was in a strong growth trajectory with a customer who would continue to order if they could continue to create value and develop their business model together with the customer. They needed to continue to reduce their previous bottlenecks and ensure that material supply worked, that the structure of the organization improved, and that they worked with international partners more than they had previously to reduce risks in their own production as the group offered expertise in other countries.

To meet the company's challenges, it implemented an extensive initial improvement program that focused on adding value to the business model and gradually building in management. The CEO had an overall role that focused on the vision, and management was given the responsibility for boundaries, ensuring competence, motivating and helping to keep the momentum going.

It worked well in the first year but gradually a third step was also needed to ensure implementation with a backbone of a developed management structure. They conducted a management study and were able to identify which issues needed to be handled more carefully and urgently. This had a positive effect immediately while many of the larger needs had longer time horizons.

We know that a large part of the success of business model innovation projects is about how management chooses to structure design in the short and long terms using Three-Step Management. There is a clear advantage for the projects to create a picture right at the start of how it can work in the longer term, which is where we choose to focus on the organization, planning, and ongoing control. This often happens at the same time that the company has ongoing business and can gradually take a position on how future plans are drawn up.

Step One is to appoint a leader for the project (often synonymous with CEO or some other decision-maker depending on what the project relates to) who will lead through others at different levels. This often differs from the regular assignment as manager. The most successful teams have a leader who is privy to the task, inclusive, and able to create a sense of the team, which motivates them to analyze, identify, and change. The person needs to focus on the opportunities, be able to freely recruit key people to a management team, and have the opportunity to reduce risks. The role also includes responsibility to create the structure for the program and identify any legacies from managers who can slow down the speed of an upcoming implementation or stop it completely. An important part of any major company are the stories and these can quite easily become self-fulfilling prophecies, so it is important to highlight this at the start if there are negative experiences.

In Step Two, it is primarily the collaboration that is in focus. The leader from Step One will assure their organization and very often it involves people directly from the C-suite. It is a team of people who work to ensure that there are resources, can motivate based on the leader's message, create frameworks, clarify schedules, and move the project forward. It is also from here that the help comes when we carry out studies where a dedicated person is available as a resource to inform about purpose, book interview times, arrange a suitable place where the interviews can be conducted, and continuously keep in touch with us through the project. This is a person who really drives the train of the innovation project forward. When the train engineer and conductor are driving toward a specific destination, the rails need to work, the gears are controlled from a control room, the signals work, and the roadside gates obstruct cars and road users to prevent accidents. There are many simpler improvements that can be made to a rail, but if the goods need to be moved a few kilometers further away, then new rails need to be laid or transported in another way for the last bit. For the companies, it is often the same with a need to identify simpler improve-ments or more extensive ones.

> *The international company was the market leader in its segments. In the most recent years, they had added businesses, broadened their range, and changed their business model several times. The Nordic operations (an important part of the international group) had a leading function for three countries and managed the control.*
>
> *The working methodology for management had been affected in recent years with a growing criticism mainly related to the fact that the company lost some key customers and the future was uncertain. In addition, there was a further acquisition underway that would support the main services and products with service, but according to rumor, the company was up almost double in volume and the CEO would get a leading position.*
>
> *The company conducted initial talks and created a project organiza-tion to handle upcoming questions. The person in charge of the pro-ject was appointed and an organization that would motivate, create resources, and work on clarifications in parallel as a comprehensive study was planned and carried out. The ambition was to get more answers from the market and customers and be able to improve and develop the plat-form. When the study was completed, several seminars were conducted and it became clearer how the project should be carried out. The project team then appointed a third level that would act as ambassadors and ensure implementation. They created a backbone with an implementa-tion team, where there was also an external consultant to help bring back experience and show how they could manage resistance and build trust.*

Step Three is about the project organization's support in explaining and creating clarity in an implementation. This is where those who have been appointed by the organization who proceed by creating in-depth goals and simplifying things become known as ambassadors. If it is a medium-sized company, it can be the department heads but also handpicked people who can listen, explain, or just be there when needed to connect with the employees. Most implementations include behavioral changes, and there-fore it is important to follow the projects more closely and offer people who can support with answering upcoming questions, correct behaviors that are contrary to creating change, and be trusted motivators. This group follows the projects that were created after the study, does regular follow-ups, and meets with team management regularly for reconciliations. They also create joint meetings within Steps One to Three in some seminars to possibly com-ment on messages, behaviors, and strengthen positive signals.

> *The medium-sized company had been successful for many years with its services and now wanted to strengthen and clarify its business by adding*

certain additional services that customers had requested in recent years. The company's business model worked well, but there were questions about whether today's management could handle a change.

The company had a clear management structure for organization, planning, and control. Senior individuals also had extensive experience in running complex and challenging projects. At the same time, they felt that it was difficult to run internal projects where very many were experts and where collaboration was not prioritized first.

The company decided to bring in help to conduct initial talks, a study, and seminars. In order to clarify tasks and roles in the project, a leader, a team, and ambassadors were sketched in from the beginning. It was a solid project that led to more inclusive and better relationships. Several additional services could be added and turnover/profits increased.

The best innovation programs are managed on an ongoing basis but with clear guidelines for what can be implemented directly in connection with initial conversations and review of the existing business model to reduce resistance and increase efficiency. We have noticed that the projects are given strength by Three-Step Management and, above all, that it creates peace and quiet for the companies so that they can see and understand how a project will be handled in the future. Many of the larger projects have had tangible shortcomings and real bottlenecks usually related to rapid growth. In these systems, the structure takes on the role of the starting the healing because the company now shows that they intend to do something for real and it contributes positively even if it does not actually relieve much at the outset.

Our view is also that Three-Step Management helps to save time as meetings are predetermined and the content is allowed to grow gradually. We see that planning contributes to fewer meetings when business model adventure projects later improve the business model. Meetings are needed to inform and share, but today they can be part of a hybrid way of working and does not always have to be live.

Insights for Three-Step Management

1. Focus on the organization, planning, and ongoing control
2. Step One is to appoint a leader for the project
3. Step Two is to focus on collaboration with the team
4. Step Three is to secure ambassadors
5. Save time, meetings are predetermined, and content grows gradually

Summary

In times when change is necessary to improve a business, management plays a key role. Not only does this refer to the individuals who lead a company, but it also refers to those who oversee and contribute both to the day-to-day running of the company and contribute to the changes as they come through the change process. When entering a new situation, it is important to understand that new managers today are expected to have greater insight and knowledge from day one when compared to older generations of managers who learned as they went along. The process of starting change is often simplified when the CEO is included in the decision-making chain right from the start, when they acknowledge the legacy of the leaders who came before, and when those companies who do this handle that legacy in an open and inclusive way. Great gains can be made in customer management if companies can identify future valuable needs and if time is given to anchor projects before they start so that there is clarity in the intents and purpose of the project.

As projects for change get underway, clarifying the business model is of utmost importance. It is crucial to have management make it clear that they stand behind the decisions that are made and that they harmonize messages and behaviors throughout the change process. In this way, they will nurture an environment where performance grows through loyalty. All leading people who are part of a business innovation (leaders, management team, and ambassadors) need to lead by example and communicate that time may be needed to create alternative behaviors and that the change will then be more lasting and profitable. This includes getting help where needed to help with fostering this understanding and identifying any bottlenecks or obstructive behaviors by thinking things through and planning well. By having an increased awareness of the business model, it creates creativity and better values, so that when using the success factors as a mirror it can generate a focus on the content when development seminars are conducted.

Managers are critical when fostering an open and creative change environment and being present every step of the way through the process. By putting the focus on generating open solutions, it gives management a sense of a freer approach and can therefore strengthen self-esteem. From this place of power, it means that managers offer an openness around materials; give access to employees, customers, partners; and identify experts to any of the support team that come in to facilitate change. On several occasions they have offered to serve as reverse mentors at traditional seminars and in specialized focus groups, and in doing so, management gives confidence in creativity and proximity in problem-solving and inspires their teams to dare to be brave as questions are asked on gradual internal and external resistance. Simpler changes can be decentralized almost immediately (a bottleneck that is often visibly identified and be rectified with minor corrections), while slightly larger changes need to be formalized, discussed, and later decided on in the right decision forum where economic assessments can motivate and ensure innovation.

The key thing that leaders can do to ensure that changes are taken up by their team and sustained into the future is to lead through others. In the beginning, it is important that the managers and leadership team listen and are involved in clarifying the purpose of the project, while initial talks serve as a support. When empowering the team throughout the process of change, it happens most painlessly when management performs a seminar where employees can speak freely to provide important feedback, after which a determination can be made on whether more analysis is needed or if there is enough information to proceed with a study. Leaders need to be able to listen and lead the way through deeper understanding and confirmation by not being swayed by all the reactions that may occur as change begins, as this may be a response to inherited behaviors in previous tasks. Help from the leadership can be critical if they can get their groups to think about issues that are identified and on the attitude of the employees. The various levels of management receive support from the top of the ladder down to the managers who are a few rungs below, so it is key that those spearheading the change can provide confidence and clarity to those supporting from below.

For managers to have the sustained effort required for making meaningful change, there is a lot to be gained in using the Three-Step Management model. There is a clear advantage for the project to create a picture right at the point where the focus on organization, planning, and ongoing control is chosen. Step One is where leaders are appointed for the project, most often the CEO or other decision-maker depending on what the project relates to. It is essential that this individual is someone who can lead through others at different levels throughout the chain. Successful projects have a leader who is tuned into the task at hand, inclusive and able to create a strong sense of the team to analyze, identify, and move toward change. They also need to be able to focus on opportunities, recruit people freely who will work as part of the management team and can reduce risks.

Step Two is primarily a collaboration that is focused on the task at hand. This is where a team of people will work to ensure that there are resources available to support the change and that they can motivate based on the leadership's message, create frameworks, clarify schedules, and move the project forward. Finally, Step Three is where ambassadors are brought in, chosen from the company, who create participation in the new structure, clarify what should be done, and work to create in-depth goals and simplify the path forward. These movements can include behavioral changes, which makes it important to follow the projects more closely as they are introduced into the revised business model. When done successfully, the best projects are managed on an ongoing basis with clear guidelines as to what can be implemented directly. This Three-Step Management model helps to save time because meetings are predetermined and the content is allowed to grow gradually.

When engaging in change, there are so many human factors to be taken into account. While some may focus on which departments are critical or who the linchpin people may be, those who are able to step back and take in the whole picture are able to see that every person has a part to play in innovating and moving in the direction of real change. Management teams who can act as a guide, sounding board, and captain all at the same time, while exercising different forms of management, inspire not only change but also the people who can take a project over the finish line in generating lasting positive change.

Notes

1 Kevin Webb, "From the Internet to the iPhone, Here Are the 20 Most Important Inventions of the Last 30 Years," *Insider*, May 17, 2019, https://www.business insider.com/most-important-inventions-of-last-30-years-internet-iphone-netflix-facebook-google-2019-5?op=1&r=US&IR=T.
2 Peter Vanham, "A Brief History of Globalization," Geo Economics, World Economic Forum, January 17, 2019, https://www.weforum.org/agenda/2019/01/how-globalization-4-0-fits-into-the-history-of-globalization/.
3 Dagny Dukach, "Research Roundup: How Technology Is Transforming Work," *Harvard Business Review*, November 7, 2022, https://hbr.org/2022/11/research-roundup-how-technology-is-transforming-work.
4 Dominique Turpin, "Top Leadership Qualities in Today's Unpredictable World," IMD, April 2016, https://www.imd.org/research-knowledge/articles/top-leadership-qualities-in-todays-unpredictable-world/.
5 Marcy Farrell, "Data and Intuition: Good Decisions Need Both," Harvard Business Publishing Corporate Learning, January 6, 2023, https://www.harvardbusiness.org/data-and-intuition-good-decisions-need-both/.
6 Turpin, "Top Leadership Qualities in Today's Unpredictable World."
7 Farrell, Data and Intuition: Good Decisions Need Both."
8 Turpin, "Top Leadership Qualities in Today's Unpredictable World."
9 Linda Hill and Kent Lineback, "Good Managers Lead Through a Team," *Harvard Business Review*, April 3, 2012, https://hbr.org/2012/04/good-managers-lead-through-a-t.
10 Webb, "From the Internet to the iPhone, Here Are the 20 Most Important Inventions of the Last 30 Years."
11 Joost Minnaar, "How Real Leaders Melt the Iceberg of Ignorance with Humility," *Corporate Rebels*, May 26, 2018, https://www.corporate-rebels.com/blog/iceberg-of-ignorance.

Chapter 6

Organizational structure

The fifth theme to account for during an innovation project is the organizational structure. Every business starts out as an idea and then over time develops the ways of working and an organization that allows it to function. Over time, these processes and procedures can become stagnant and ingrained in such a way that creativity is stifled. Taking apart the structure in the process of change to see how it works and where it can be improved allows for rejuvenation and new opportunities for efficiency.

The internal structure as security and support for implementation

The organizational structures of large and medium-sized enterprises have changed over the past 40 years, in line with increased globalization and internationalization.[1] The structure of an organization describes how work is created and the flow in a business model (solution) that helps groups work on individual tasks.[2] The more traditional solutions stem from clear capabilities with clear roles, specialization, and helping teams/departments scale operations. The four most common forms have been function, division, flat, and matrix, but today there are significantly more forms with regions, products, teams, networks, and sometimes a mixture of some of these.[3] With today's flow of information, we see more virtual and network opportunities and companies are trying to open up to more flexible options. There are advantages and disadvantages in all forms in terms of how best to use them in a business model, which means that strong companies should consistently seek to evolve to find the best solution for them. There are many challenges for today's global companies and with the winds changing direction quickly it is crucial to be prepared for rapid changes without losing the long-term focus.

We have seen that the business innovation projects are very dependent on the structure of the organization and how it delivers data to the projects. An additional perspective is that the structure should create suitable

DOI: 10.4324/9781003402121-6

conditions for the business model's value creation and provide the best possible conditions and deliveries. As companies grow larger, there are often many groups, units, or departments in an organization to ensure that all aspects of the business are covered in the most efficient way. In order for it to be possible to lead and control units, strategies are needed that have goals and metrics. In some of the multinational business models, there can also be several units in different countries, and there are often very complex solutions that need to be updated, trimmed, and developed. The structure describes all of these elements and holds all units together with appropriate systems that allow for goals that can be measured. The business model innovation cases depend on all systems and the data become available during the first steps when the business model is mapped and later when the projects are analyzed and planned. After that, the company makes decisions about any improvements or corrections in the business model and then both the system and the organization can be part of a change process.

Most of today's systems are adapted specifically for each individual organization, which often means that it is costly and time-consuming if change is implemented too early. We see that it has become easier to access datasets and sometimes it can be especially important with productivity analyses in connection with mapping bottlenecks. In general, it has become easier for all users to use the systems and the previous issue of data maturity is now more about data storage and data security. The internal structure needs to serve as a security and support for projects that will improve and change business models.

The company had grown from a smaller organization in the 1990s to nearly 150 employees in three business areas with different specialties. They had also established operations abroad. The different areas were governed with their own systems, but the organizations were combined for administration, HR, and finance with an overall holding.

It worked, but as the company grew, the company felt that the business areas needed more input from each business system and thought about whether these could be linked to a management system or if there was an alternative enterprise resource planning (ERP) system with different modules for their industry. The control worked mostly because the management was experienced, but they experienced a greater need for digitization and further knowledge of the possibilities.

They established one-to-one mentoring meetings to begin a change project during a set period and enabled alternative thinking. After a year, they had appointed two new younger management members for two of the three business areas and also started the purchase of a new business system and the business went forward.

We see that business model innovation programs are dependent on data support to be able to get a better and safer change process that will build toward increased growth. It requires that the organization works efficiently and has a strong record of success before larger projects begin. Leaders look at needs differently than those who are perhaps further down the chain in the organization, but in order to support business and innovation projects, it is an advantage if the available data is the best possible for that company. It is costly and usually too time-consuming to speed up data development that will support an organizational structure; therefore, good evidence is needed to be able to trust what situation exists at the outset.

Many large and midsize companies have business solutions where the systems that the organization uses are owned by a system supplier who can easily offer more secure data management overall. In this system, regular software updates are made and there is often flexibility built in that allows the structure to change gradually, but major changes often require different time intervals depending on which systems and which languages are impacted. The structure is an important element, but, above all, the project often has incipient bottlenecks or wants to seek completely new markets and so all aspects must be included. Leadership should be able to trust the systems and use programs that are secure and can be followed up.

The company delivered data solutions to a special niche and had customers all over the world. The business model was a business system for operations focused on three different segments in the same industry. They were built with modules, and customers could influence appearance and usability themselves, but at an additional cost.

They received ongoing new software updates in two main languages (English and German) and there was a user group even among the largest customers that the company supported. The company needed to improve their interactions with customers and go through alternative channels and, therefore, also change part of the existing business model.

They started conversations with one-to-one meetings that developed into a comprehensive needs analysis of customers with greater needs. As a result, the company developed a new module for CRM that could also be offered to customers. A central issue became the user perspective and several experts were asked to participate in a number of focus groups that were carried out with the UX concept as a need-driven area of concern.

We see that the existing form of how a company works affects the projects both directly in the control of the project and indirectly with possible planning and communication. When the projects are established, it is not uncommon for the first meetings to be more about the organization than about the focus of the business model. The internal flow is important but a business model starts with the segment, the market, the customer, and ends in a delivery. The impact can be about reporting, opinions of management, various system solutions within the company, external experts, routines that need to be trimmed, lack of competence, quality deficiencies, and many more aspects. The beginning is facilitated if the communication from the project owners of an innovation project see the possibilities and can already communicate how the existing structure will help the project and that it constitutes a security for a future implementation.

The company had gone through an organizational change to strengthen its business model, from different operations to regions which would simplify the customer process for the larger customers. The change meant that the group lost some local expertise, but compensated it with overall support for the larger business, review of documentation, and a controller and now could attract more competent employees.

The criticism was that they were slowing down and the new employees who were supposed to facilitate processes with central agreements had problems because the computer systems were not ready when the organization was launched. Several of them were recruited from larger companies and were willing to work with data governance but instead they now had to work with considerations that were lacking and were completely dependent on manual decisions.

The launch had been postponed for several months and therefore an innovation project was started to support the change in real time to get things ready to go. After a few months of one-to-one meetings, the company had hired similar external services and started an internal qualitative study to motivate and clarify the new organizational structure further.

For the projects, we know that it is mostly about understanding what conditions the structure can offer to strengthen analysis, seminars, and implementation. It is an important issue for the existing business model and an improved one. We see that many newer projects are happy to work more flexibly, which also means a new working situation for individuals and groups. Today's new systems allow many people to talk on a platform at the same time as an image transfer takes place, which simplifies processes and gives individuals greater flexibility. For the change projects, these systems can be positive and we have used online solutions for interviews, seminars, and major training efforts, which has worked well. It is especially beneficial when the distances are longer or when people have difficulty participating in person and hence we have chosen this new technology together with these companies. The last years of the COVID-19 pandemic have shown that technology has expanded the abilities of remote communication and kept the organizations going for those who were in a position to keep their jobs.

Insights for security and support

1. Support from systems for a safer process
2. Perform an inventory to understand the structure in the model
3. Explain the projects use of the structure
4. Focus on the important data that can bring value
5. Look for flexibility and user-friendly solutions

The need for organizational structure to be anchored with the leader and other managers

For medium and large companies working in an international market, questions about structure and organization are often part of overall conversations about business systems. Therefore, it is often a question of building or rebuilding vital parts of a business model when it comes to a change to an existing structure.[4] The technical aids have developed rapidly and today many of the systems can be offered in several local languages, but companies still often choose a central language for the company, which often becomes English. Technology issues are often large investments in the beginning, but system suppliers also offer different types of payment solutions in everything from buying, program rental, user solutions, and subscribing. As companies expand their business, the structure and organization also need to be flexible and scalable. Therefore, companies are looking for solutions that are able to provide cost advantages, better margins, and with lower risks. As it has become cheaper, the hardware has decreased in importance, and today, it is the systems, security, and how the companies store data that are in focus. It is possible to choose systems in the same way as cars are chosen, in different price ranges, with different fuels, with additional features, and with safer more well-tested tires.

If the business model changes, the ultimate scenario is that it is anchored in several levels and that the different levels are given enough time for understanding to be shared and available computer system can be used to reinforce the messages of why and what contribution this should make. It is about making uniform main messages but also later allowing adoption of information how the project is communicated. People's adaptability is often a mirror image of how clear the path forward is and whether the team can handle the change. It makes it easier if there are people in the organization who can function as support, listen to questions, and clarify messages while being good role models. A change in a business model usually also involves an adaptation or change in the structure of the organization, which affects everyone who belongs to the solution.

The structure is the train rails, the systems are the trains that run at different speeds, and the carriages are the organization that transports goods and people to different destinations. A change in the structure of a business model may involve all or part of a group. It has been the case that system changes or system extensions have been part of the implementation. Management needs to see the existing systems as a certainty that the project can gradually develop with the available data via the systems, interviews, focus groups, and surveys.

In all that work, the most important thing is that there is an anchoring in the company for the project, but it is unusual for there to be a change of system during that period. The organizational forms are tools for creating images of how the company works, how the work is divided, who is included, and how they relate to each other.

The international market-leading company had changed its business model continuously in recent years due to COVID-19 and this had led to layoffs and terminations. It took a lot to access data to create an overview and create uniform messages from owners, employees, partners, and customers.

The anchoring in the central functions went fast due to the emergency situation and therefore when most of it had fallen into place in the organization, there was a feeling that some questions needed to be dealt with again and a clarification was required for those who had been rehired as well as for several new employees.

The anchoring was carried out with individual interviews, seminars, and subsequent training seminars. They gathered in small groups and identified issues that needed to be explained or would become important moving forward. In order for it to work, the initial meetings were conducted on different days. After that, everyone gathered and provided feedback on what all the seminars had gone through and planned. Pre-anchoring was very successful.

The internal structure needs to upgrade consistently and the leaders need to be clear that they are behind the data, key figures, and any change leaders. When the change is planned, people still can't always relate to what's to come; therefore, the timing of the change is also sensitive once it happens. We have seen leaders who have been very surprised by all the reactions that have come out as changes were implemented and had to explain that it is not uncommon. On the contrary, if the anchoring is handled with more messages in more channels and managers/leaders are available for questions, it usually goes painlessly.

There should be meetings that relate to reconciliation and it is also important that milestones are reported back to increase confidence in change and growth. It helps the new organization understand the progress and gives a feeling of security. This responsibility exists for the leader of a business model innovation project but is always managed by their team. We usually emphasize that all parts are equally important in a model and that the company is careful with clarity, information, and communicates in several channels. Communication needs to be mixed with images and written words and ideally culminate with meetings. If possible, communication can be repeated and include good examples.

The international company had increased revenue dramatically over the past five years, which meant that after this time of expansion there were some limitations on continued growth.

They needed to get a better flow and clarify how responsibility would be shared and who was actually responsible for each segment and product. Production took place in different parts of the world, but coordination was assumed in one flow. Management reasoned that the previously flexible structure was not enough to make more rational decisions in the value chain. They started a business model innovation project with initial talks and a comprehensive internal study with subsequent seminars.

It showed that the sales organization was active, the brand increased in awareness, the older employees had to take on great responsibility, awareness of the concept of processes was low, there was a lack of a control system, there was ambiguity about the limits of decisions, and the management's time was not enough. The business model was corrected over six months with clear governance processes, which were established in a checklist, and created an organization with main processes and complimentary support processes.

Despite the size of companies, several of our projects show that the organizational structure is often an inherited sketch that has developed in line with market expectations. The organization develops both naturally over time and when there are changes of different leaders within the companies. We also perceive that today's access to information and communication in modern society positively affects the structure faster than before with both short- and long-term effects when driving forces increase and create potential bottlenecks. This means that the management needs to be more observant of their business and how the structure affects the ability to deliver according to customers' wishes. In the early development seminars, we analyze the existing model and the organization's structure and work together on various improvement proposals.

The midsize company's operations had a good reputation, good location, clear direction, the right staff, and a flat organization. They worked intensively to maintain and raise the educational quality, which contributed to satisfied customers and a good reputation.

The company's challenge was in the system, the structure, and how they could continue to develop the organization for their business. They felt that customers demanded different opening hours, a more flexible solution, and more transparency, but they had difficulty meeting these requests.

They conducted a qualitative study and five internal seminars with the ambition to better meet customers' expectations, improve their business model, and make the necessary adjustments in the organizational structure and in the work organization. This led to changes in opening hours, smarter planning, and some additional managers who could support and develop educational issues and ensure that the culture also applied to temporary staff, something that was initially lacking and proved to be a shortcoming in all briefings. The combined relationships of customers, external partners, and in the internal work organization were good, but with the projects it became even stronger and value creation ended up as a focus in the anchoring.

A business model contains many different parts and customer perceptions are important to be able to build value and later also choose the best possible structure that can meet these desires. If a business model innovation case involves radical changes, it will be better motivated and simplified if there are people in the groups who are social and positive about not only the ideas and the company but also themselves. The leader in an innovation case should ensure that the team works to ensure that the solution is value-creating and realistic, the anchoring is broad, the work with the change takes place in stages, the messages are harmonized for increased understanding and that there are ambassadors who can answer questions to create motivation instead of doubt and resistance.

Insights for anchoring with leaders

1. The team presents a value-creation plan including ambassador
2. Secure the effects on the structure and make an inventory
3. Reconciliation and important milestones, plan seminars
4. Communication plan with overall message
5. Pursue radical changes and create social groups for implementation

Focus on the variables for speed

The new methods of electronic communications have increased the ability of people to communicate and to inform themselves. The increased trade and movement of capital between countries have driven a development where organizations have become more efficient. The visionary leaders have had a great need to scale the structures within their businesses and gradually build larger organizations with more people. In that change, it has been at least as important to develop functioning processes, smart and changing systems, refined and well-thought-out communication, elaborate tools and instructions for information transfer, and have a clear idea of management. These variables are central to scaling systems and building business more successfully.

The international companies benefit from the fact that the three parameters of nations, companies, and people interact. They can go a little further in their solutions in looking for the best possible resource and then develop the model with more actors in the structure. In this, there is also an insight that the models need to be commercialized faster and preferably make ongoing changes or short efforts.[5] It is about the company focusing on opportunities and everything that can improve with the help of resources and digitalization. It's about getting closer to data and communicating more internally and with the customer. It is about seeing the processes as radio waves for us to be able to listen to the radio or that it is 5G so that we can talk faster, safer, and be more sustainable in the future when we are using our mobiles.[6,7]

In business model innovation projects, improvements and quality assurance are always pointing toward upcoming projects in a pending action plan. There are quick profits if the company can analyze its article registers and remove older spare parts for products that they no longer need to store. There are quick wins if the quality department can create documents for certain processes that people otherwise need to go and ask about. It can be about a personnel manual that has not been updated and therefore the new employees do not receive the information that they should have. There are often long lists in our creative seminars when we go through conclusions of the various studies. For the management team, these may be completely unknown issues, although they may seem obvious. The structural questions that most organizations wrestle with are about how the efficiency of the organization works, what the division of labor looks like, observance of coordination of processes, determining whether some of the processes are more rational, and at the same time when they do not work, and when or where bottlenecks arise.

It is usually the variables that determine how quickly the organization can manage its development as customer orders increase. In an innovation process, it is therefore important to include all three perspectives and solve the structure perplexity – the variables, the human element, and the strategic piece. Since a business model can also be built in many different ways, it is good to try to decide how it should be assessed and what driving forces influenced these three horizons. Most larger companies measure effects and build reports, but when reviewing structure perplexity by weighing more perspectives, analyses often show that measurement rather reduces flexibility.

> *The large international company was a major player that operated in many markets worldwide. Over the years, they had grown mainly through company acquisitions that later enabled different arrangements for products, structures, and new business models to emerge. They had a good eye for different segments, customers on all continents, building relationships, and offered their solutions in different channels. Their manufacturing company was primarily governed by a mixture of focus on products where there was a far-reaching authorization for research and development of the channels creatively.*
>
> *In the Swedish branch of the organization, which covered large parts of the Nordic region, manufacturing worked worse than in other regions. They had started changes several times in the past but each time it stopped due to a lack of key employees in the factories. Therefore, it was decided that the company would analyze the organization and all the variables that bound the structure together, including the human element and the structural baseline. They started with one-to-one meetings for a whole year and then proceeded with a larger qualitative study.*
>
> *It showed that the company suffered from cultural problems and that the structural issues never turned into a highway for growth. This meant that it was not a matter of lack of a certain competence but a far-reaching lack of adaptation of the business model. The entire production was driven by an earlier variant of the business solution and therefore a structure perplexity arose in the form of a clash between the structure and the human element with strategies that worked for the wrong business model. This led to the fact that the owner company decided to change the direction of the company and move production to another country and reshaped the company to include only a sales organization with administration in an alternate country.*

Most of the variables can be controlled in existing systems in medium and large companies, but when a changed business model is created, it can mean questions that deal with changes in everything, from systems, management, information, communication, quality, and the like, will arise. Large and midsize companies have different abilities to see opportunities and many times it is governed by these underlying variables and how the companies create reports and make decisions. We have been through a number of radical processes where the costs to change the opportunities to access more relevant data for the new business have become very large.

For an innovation design, it is important that there is a backup and trust in the existing systems that often participate or directly build the processes in the companies. Sometimes we have created some simple exercises in the problem seminars after the studies to show how a process can work or what happens when it does not. In many cases, we usually use the salary process and demonstrate what happens when things go wrong if salaries are not paid. The payroll process is based on a contract with the employee and shows how the person works, how time is reported, how it is managed in administration, and how a salary is made and finally paid minus any tax plus any surcharges. The interesting thing is that companies have a lot of processes, more than most employees think of and know about.

In recent years, the company had won several large contracts and the organization had grown with different operations, and today there were ten operations with different orientations. The number of employees had also passed 50 permanent employees and they had recruited many part-time employees. The competitive situation was good and several customer groups were in the pipeline.

The atmosphere was generally good, but there were shortcomings in the organization's governance and among staff who expressed that the internal communication did not work and that it could become an issue externally as well. The company decided to make an inventory of the entire business and started an innovation project. They conducted initial talks and a review of the existing business model.

This led to short-term clarifications in the internal information and internal communication systems and indicated that some customers needed more support. Subsequently, several studies were carried out within an internal project in nine stages, which were created for the project. The various studies that were performed helped to make opportunities visible, improved margins, focused on the management of the individual business and how they would interact, the actors in the model, different profit centers that turned into one and a clearer delivery. The project lasted for two years with a nice development of the company and the structure now worked delicately with new improved strategies to the revised deal.

Focusing on different processes and how they are handled in the existing systems allows for a better outcome later in the qualitative study. If the necessary processes for information and communication are missing or deficient, it is an advantage to improve these before a project starts. In order for a business and innovation project to be truly successful/developed/transferred to, it is necessary to have a central system and process questions. This development of the central system and processing of questions describes how the structure combines with the organization and the workflow. For the included projects that are financially validated, a risk assessment should also be able to assess the credibility of their success. In order to keep the momentum going in the projects, IT and managers needs to support the risk.

The midsize company had created a full-service solution in its field, which meant a fairly extensive change in the business. It would have meant quite big changes in the entire business model and take both effort and time away from the organization. The new business model meant a greater commitment in the respective partial delivery.

In order for the company to achieve success, it was important to move some of the manual processes into systems and at the same time improve all the variables substantially that would affect a collaboration with the larger customers. A build-up of various systems began in all areas, several key figures were studied, new meetings were created, and internal routines for reports were built and gradually the company started developing innovation projects.

It went better and better in line with new customers in the three main areas. Collaborations with larger customers also meant that their own routines were challenged and improved. The company continued to invest in structure, systems, and to make better use of the variables than before.

The array of variables that create leverage for the projects and generate the company's growth may outnumber those we have indicated. The important ones are those that identify what development is possible and what will streamline and optimize processes. An optimization here means that if the variable was not used more than required then it should be streamlined and developed. The ambition is to find the processes that can be improved dynamically and contribute to a faster road, a highway, that can handle more cars in different lanes at different speeds.

Management and leadership of the innovation projects, together with those who own IT, need to influence the way of thinking about opportunities and everything that can bring about improvements regarding digitalization. It's about getting the speed up but not driving off the road and making sure the car has enough energy to get to the next filling station.

Insights for variables for speed

1. Influence the way of thinking about opportunities (inventory)
2. Focus on different processes for a better outcome (search)
3. Develop central system and process questions
4. Backup and trust in the existing systems
5. Make a risk assessment (credibility)

The process connected to the projects

The globalized market has improved the living conditions of many people around the world but it also meant a certain specialization of specific countries in regard to production/industry and that other countries have become more raw material suppliers.[8] Banks and multinational companies have been the driving force in this development and made the world appear larger than the borders of individual countries. To make it work, several institutions have been created and laws have been put in place to simplify the export and import of goods and services. Right now, in the aftermath of the COVID-19 pandemic, we are also living through more global crises with uncertainty that creates inflation and higher interest rates. It is a time where globalization is shaking its foundations but, at the same time, world leaders continue to move forward incessantly. The external and internal driving forces affect business models, structure, organization, and processes, which ultimately entail risks of poorer deliveries or ultimately no deliveries at all for several companies.

Process is a chain of related activities – it consists of a structure and a result (object). It is usually described as the total activities including the start right through to the end. In addition, a process is used over and over again. The whole idea is to create co-understanding, contribute to a common way of working and enable efficiency and improvement. When a business model changes its process, it also usually means a new design of the company's structure and organization.[9] Because a business model describes how the company creates value over and over again, it describes what is done, how the process creates value, turns the perspective to the recipient, contributes with a holistic perspective, allows effective control, and can simplify and show how it works between the different actors in the process.

In a functional solution, most commonly and historically speaking, companies create a number of main processes for the customer's management and in these there are several sub-processes that contain components and manual reconciliation points. This creates a business process that can show a logical solution and at the same time explain the different steps that bind the entire chain together. The logical solution shows several work processes that should then be supported strategically by overall processes that relate to longer planning, global and work environment and by support processes that include marketing, communication, finance, IT, HR, R&D, and finance. The numbers may differ depending on the company's history and the influence of the owner groups.

Other terms can be core processes, support processes, and management processes that are used to control and lead core and support processes. There are many receivers for processes who can be internal and external, such as customers, suppliers, employees, society, owners, authorities, customers, management, and certainly many more. In the longer projects, it is interesting to see how these organizations handle their value creation in the model and how they adapt later when it is improved or they develop something completely new.

The company was one of the largest in a large group and had been around for a long time, serving as a role model for other companies in the group. They had worked for a long time to refine and develop their customer segment, handled certain customer groups extremely closely, and developed knowledge of their needs. This included building in channels and creating a business model with clear value and the correct structure for their business. The organization's structure was based on a developed customer process that started with project planning and purchasing, then switched to an advanced service production with reconciliations that were handled by quality control and logistics in the end. In each part of the process there were also clear parts with various computerized reconciliations.

Now two sister companies wanted to use the company as a mirror to develop their own businesses. The company had demanded that they could also develop new areas at the same time and be able to benefit from the joint process as the sister companies paid for the mirroring of the company. A joint project was created with business meetings and then a controlled study of the two sister companies' existing business model was carried out.

There were some initial improvements in customer management and on the delivery side. Then a joint customer and employee study was conducted. Based on this, the two sister companies were able to create similar processes and a new area of interest for the company from these two companies. They conducted ten joint seminars and in total the project lasted two years. The three companies had increased their turnover by over 20 percent in terms of company and 30 percent in profits.

We see that when the crucial processes have been important and of significance for several companies in terms of organizational structure, it has mainly been about there being a preparation and understanding, an organization that is digitized and optimized and has a clear agreement with its customer to create a unique value. At the same time, it has been important that the entire business model has had clarity, that the business model develops new clear value and that the business can be developed continuously. The processes have also contributed to strategies being implemented on an ongoing basis and where they are anchored well, they create more understanding of the organization. This happens continuously together with the existing business.

The large group was divided into a number of regions with six companies where each company had a full production, including R&D, marketing, production, and administration. They had high goals and ongoing follow-ups of both customers and their own staff. For several years they had advanced their internal goals and felt wind in their sails.

The company had received many external awards for quality development, fine products, good deliveries, and best company recognition. However, in the past year, the quality of one of the larger services that included several subcontractors had faltered and complaints increased. They had training with all suppliers that focused on service quality, but their customers had raised the goals for measurement and several of the suppliers did not meet the requirements.

The company started a business model innovation project that included all services so as not to single one out and conducted both internal and external interviews in a comprehensive study. It showed that the company, despite very good grades, had a bottleneck of this service and the potential for improvement was good in the process. They developed a closer solution to the organization and regained trust through significant improvements along with the largest customers. The project lasted a year.

The leader and team in the business model innovation projects should always have a focus on the business model and how it creates value for the customer. A good process geared toward the customer has a clear and distinct segmentation with great customer knowledge in regard to expectations, preferences, and an understanding of what is the best possible outcome for the customer. It is about directing the process toward the customer with a close relationship, involving bringing out a need and ensuring that the expected value chain lasts from start to finish. Customer interactions should be ongoing, solution-oriented, and ideally proactive. The whole customer process is geared toward delivering value, along with simple, vibrant, and talking strategies. It is about creating common positive experiences that benefit both parties, the customer and everyone involved in the delivery.

Over the past 20 years, the company had continued to develop system solutions for the international market and the products had become more and more popular. Customers were located all over the world in a number of segments.

They made ongoing adjustments in the market to check the current and future customer needs. They decided to start one-to-one meetings and then performed a qualitative study with the CEOs in several of the largest companies in the segments. It showed that the company had a good position and good competitiveness for future needs.

Subsequent seminars focused on both preventive measures and creating new offerings within the system as modules. The project lasted two years and both sales and earnings increased by almost 50 percent from start to finish. A lot of it was about targeting more active sales and offering alternative payment solutions.

The interpretation of needs should allow the processes to be able to strengthen and contribute to the customer, but it takes people time to understand and be able to draw conclusions. It is clear that it requires reflection, planning both overall and in detail and, above all, insights into customer needs. Leadership is an important factor together with market knowledge, especially for the business model. If the projects are based on leading through others at three distinct levels that collaborate but act with different roles and tasks, the company is well equipped for a profitable journey.

The best companies have analyzed the market carefully, chosen the focus of customer area, and then checked all the key resources to be able to build the particular product or market the unique service together with others. They generally spend more time than others understanding how the products can be developed over time along with elaborate strategies. It is probably the most central process for success to be able to develop abilities and an outstanding delivery.

Insights for the process connected to the projects

1. Learn from the company's customer process (market, segment, value)
2. Create a strength and weakness analysis of the structure
3. Direct the process toward the customer
4. Describe an overall process including details and insight
5. The management needs to secure the value creation

Serves as a decision support

Technological development will continue with emerging technologies for questions that are important to solve from a global perspective. This will mean the development of new business models but also, above all, corrections and additions of already-existing models. Another important topic is education and jobs for the large groups of people who are going into working life in five to ten years, as generation Alpha, those born from 2010 forward, will be more than 2 billion by 2025. How will they want to live, and what technological aids will become dominant in 10, 30, or 100 years?[10]

Our method includes future exploration with a large number of parameters that can help to see trends and later create alternative scenarios when we work with the conclusions in seminars after completed studies. The total data that emerge in the innovation projects follow a decision-making process developed from our action research process: identify a purpose (problem), what factors limit production (bottlenecks), develop alternatives (the analysis in the study), analyze the options (in the subsequent seminars), implement the innovations that create value for the business model (activity plans and training seminars), and create control and development systems (lead through Two- and Three-Step Management). The projects can sometimes also contain decisions that have a different character and then they are instead strategic, tactical, or operational. There may be questions about whether they should go together with another company. Should we increase our organization? What should we do to make these two companies work together in our model? Who should we recruit? How often should we communicate this change? What should be said to consumers about our upcoming service development?

Medium-sized and large companies today have access to a lot of data in everything, from various business systems, social media, the Internet and e-mail, to name a few. It creates new opportunities but it is also important to check that the data used are actually true. Process and system operators need to be able to collaborate with decision-makers at multiple levels in companies, whether they work in the company or enter into a partnership with them. Many decisions are made every day that are a direct consequence of all the data used and therefore companies need to clarify which systems are operational and support daily operations, such as business systems, various workflow systems and CRM. Warehouses and varying online analytical processing tools provide great opportunities for companies to plan, organize, and combine their datasets in different ways.

It is the leader who drives the questions forward in the change projects and sometimes this person is the same as the regular decision-maker (CEO), and there can be confusion in what the project's decision is and what the ordinary decision to the business is. It is important to distinguish between the regular activities and the projects to clarify when there is thought and planning (which are the first steps) and when the implementation starts with action. At the same time, there are big gains in performing small corrections right away without having to wait for the go ahead to make the changes later. In the implementation of the business model innovation case, the systems primarily serve as a support for coordination, planning, certain reports, and follow-up. It is ensured by the leader, and the team appointed takes care of the contacts that are necessary later to make the required analyses.

The company functioned as a consulting company in a larger international group and they had a few hundred highly specialized employees. They supported from within the group's main business and offered support in long-term development issues with knowledge that focused on the business and overall strategies.

The challenge for the company was that the questions often "popped up" here and there and the internal consulting functions were therefore not always used systematically and relevant data were inaccessible internally or quite often required too much effort to obtain. In order to be able to coordinate the business and implement more safely, they started one-to-one meetings that focused on the business and how this would be changed with the help of existing aids.

This led to a number of strategy conferences that were part of a positioning of services and products for the company. They were represented in the large cities with operations in three main areas. They stated that they had extensive knowledge, were a nursery for future leaders, and covered very large areas. The calls and conferences showed that the company needed access to the operational data together with being able to analyze warehouses and partners.

We have noticed that the increased amount of data in recent years has also meant that it has become more difficult to analyze and that projects become dependent on general considerations. We see that secondary data help move the projects forward and serve as active support, together with interviews both inside and outside the companies. The whole process for a project becomes related to different decision-making systems and operational data; therefore, the problem inventories also become dependent on openness and a good climate. It is also about gradual feedback to the purpose that is chiseled out and coordinated in order to be later transformed into an action plan by management.

The collaboration between the process and system owners in the companies also needs to be highlighted, and if it works, the project gets more access to relevant data that can be used later in the planning for implementation. It can be data needed to evaluate segments, customer satisfaction, purchase volumes, quality controls, certain production outcomes, product deliveries, comparisons between determined volumes and outcomes, and to generate reports of various kinds. Quite commonly, companies build a vision during the work on an innovation process and also weigh in segments and expected volumes and make financial calculations. It is an extensive work to analyze combinations, solve bottlenecks in ongoing business models, and later form an implementation plan. The big point of the subsequent seminars after conducted interviews is to create a basis that improves and develops the business.

The company had experienced major changes in the market and their business model worked, but they felt that customers were demanding

solutions that they could not deliver on within the structure of the exist-
ing business model's organization. Therefore, they had begun to gather
information on all the issues surrounding agreements and what might be
important for a more comprehensive mapping.

It was a gradual effort and they had many informal contacts with
fewer number of clients who had to act as early adopters to the ideas
that were presented gradually. After an internal survey that retrieved data
from the business system and other related systems that created analyses,
the company invited about ten customers to a workshop in two rounds.
Customers were invited to bring data and in connection with the invita-
tion and a number of main points were presented for upcoming focus
groups. All invitees came to the seminars and even a number of those
not invited attended.

The work resulted in new documentation that could be processed
between meetings. After an extraordinary meeting, the company had
agreed with some of the customers to make a prototype solution with
them and made changes. The work took two years and was very success-
ful. They created a common system for planning and informing, which
also worked well to be able to make successive decisions for the com-
pany. The investments were extensive, but the results were overwhelm-
ingly positive in the end.

In the projects, there are often many variations on the same data set and
therefore it is important to have a good preplanning and the ability to stop
when it is enough. There may be both an overall purpose to the project
and some initiating questions that it should be answered more directly. An
innovation project often has rich data, which means that there is a risk that
too many issues will be discussed and this can lead to a loss of clarity in the
project. It is a difficult balancing act when the structure is to be analyzed
both culturally and strategically. The strategies should carry goals and at
the same time be measurable. It is easy to deviate from what is needed and
make adjustments in advance of the likely reactions from employees or
managers. It takes courage to analyze and implement and it is the leader,
together with the team and the ambassadors, who makes it happen and
secures the outcome. We see that companies are sometimes forced to adapt
because they set aside too little time for anchoring in implementation and
can express themselves in too few seminars in too short a time. Above all,
major changes in work methodology require an understanding of why the
previous behaviors need to change and where time is crucial to be able to
show how these changes will improve results.

The international company had experienced increased competition in
several markets along with a slight drop in the Nordic region. Some of

these conditions could be related to the economy, but there were also some questions about the direction of the business model. In particular, the company had had delays on a number of new products and some older ones could not be repaired quickly enough.

The old products were technically good but with outdated technology and even the sales tools were substandard. The company collected data and concluded that the combinations of data were insufficient.

They conducted a qualitative study to obtain more opinions from key customers, which strengthened the company. The existing system could not be developed to add attributes, but improvements were needed in the business system with a new CRM.

The best projects are better planned; have freer access to data; and have better collaboration between processes, system owners, and those who lead the projects. We see that these collaborations are more digital and more realistic in their analysis. Our view is that running and performing the analyses are demanding on companies, but with more time and more secure data, the results are positive. It is about experiences that create better abilities to be able to share better and strengthen collaborations in the ongoing business. Some leaders find it easier to create open and bold meetings that can contribute to good decision-making, while others are faster when using their own judgments, which does not always create the best outcomes. If a leader moves very quickly, quite often their decisions should be implemented later and if the analysis is not anchored, the implementation often meets with greater resistance.

Insights for decision support

1. Secure good preplanning of the data
2. Primary and secondary data work well together
3. Focus on collaboration between the process and system owners
4. Plan and solve bottlenecks in ongoing business models (rich data risk)
5. Trust the data and be brave and bold

Summary

Organizational structure allows any innovation project to have the support that it needs to grow as well as shining a light on any potential bottlenecks that may come up as the project continues. Data support is essential for carrying out a successful innovation project as it leads to a better and safer process as it helps in the understanding of what conditions within the structure can strengthen analysis, seminars, and the ultimate implementation. The reason that structure is an important element is because the project can have bottlenecks at the beginning or because the growth, which is necessary, may take place in entirely new markets. When change is undertaken, there is an existing form of how a company works and this has knock-on effects in projects both directly and indirectly. Having a solid understanding of the structure can help to avoid costly and too time-consuming processes to speed up data development to support the organizational structure as an existing system supplier can more easily offer secure data management, which will cost less in the long run. Knowledge of these existing systems will allow development, which allows many people to communicate on the same platform at the same time as the platform is handling image transfer in a more simplified way, which will give individuals greater flexibility.

As with any change project, it is critical to have an anchoring of organizational structure with the leaders who will work with and oversee the change. Any innovation case should ensure that the solution to the issues the company is facing is value-creating and realistic with broad anchoring. This will help the change to take place in stages rather than bringing in massive changes at once and will ensure that the messages are harmonized for increased understanding by the team and the ambassadors who will communicate the project as it progresses. The process of a change project allows management to be more observant of their business and to take the opportunity to understand how the structure of their enterprise affects the ability to deliver according to the demands of their customer base as well as how the natural development will lead from change, even should the leadership shift as well. The process of having regular meetings not only sets out the path of a project but also should be undertaken to understand the milestones through analyzing the timelines and when they are met. This process of reconciliation leads to an increase in confidence and growth as leaders will be clear in their understanding of the data and communicating it further with key figures and to any changes in leadership.

It is not enough to have understanding, but communication is the key as a change project gets underway. A manager who simply speaks about change may find questions arising that are difficult to explain via e-mail alone, so it is essential to use a variety of mediums to get the information of the project across using a mixture of pictures, written text, and most importantly, meetings. Being able to sit down with the team and have a dialogue will ensure that everyone is on the same page and looking in the same direction throughout the process. This symbiotic process will generate positive feelings throughout the group, which in turn will help to motivate the team as they will feel included in the process and have a good feeling about where the changes are going. This is especially important if a business model innovation case involves radical changes as it builds trust in the team about the expected outcome and will simplify the messages that will push everyone forward.

As a business model innovation case proceeds, there are many variables for speed, which can help or hinder progression toward the company's goals. Moving toward digitization provides the opportunity to see what can be brought in with new technologies and influence the way of thinking about the improvements it can bring. In many cases, this is governed by underlying variables or the variables that create leverage. It is also the key to focus on different processes and how they are handled in the existing systems and whether they allow for a better outcome later in the qualitative study. The goal is identifying the processes that can be improved dramatically and contribute to a faster road to change. The key to taking a business innovation project from a plan on paper into the real working world is for it to be able to be successfully transferred to a central system that can process questions. This will allow for further development and true success. Similarly, there must be a backup and trust in the existing system that participate or directly build the processes in the companies. By having all the variables within the structure organized and understood, projects can be financially validated, and a risk assessment will be able to assess the credibility of the success as the change evolves.

Having a thorough understanding of a company's structure will allow processes of change to be predictable and dynamic. Successful companies have their finger on the pulse of the market, have chosen their customer area, and have ensured that they have access to all the resources required to build their particular product or offer their unique services to that market. In the process of undertaking change, it is crucial to prepare and understand the structure, especially in the case where an organization is highly digitized, optimized, and has a clear agreement. The successful processes are directed forward toward the customer with close relationships that understand the need of the client paired with the ability to deliver from start to finish. This takes reflection, insight into customer needs, and a combination of macro/micro planning. The leader and their team who have a focus on the business model and how it creates value for the customer will be more reactive to the changes in the process but also proactive as far as the leadership will be key in guiding the business while also bearing in mind the variation in the market.

As a project progresses, having access to the necessary decision support ensures that proposed changes will transition into positive growth beyond the project phase. The amount of data can be difficult to analyze, which leads to projects becoming dependent on general considerations, which is why good preplanning with many variations on the same data becomes so important. Having access to secondary data helps to propel the project forward and serves as an active support along with interviews that are conducted through the project both inside and outside the companies. It cannot be underestimated that highlighting the collaboration between the process and system owners in the companies leads to increased understanding, which can be a support as the change goes on. It can take extensive work to have an excellent plan that analyzes combinations and solve bottlenecks in the ongoing business models, but this is what the most successful projects tend to have in common. The project has a rich dataset that is well organized and managed so that there is not a loss of clarity.

All in all, it takes courage to analyze and implement changes, especially when to all outward appearances things seem to be running smoothly, if not seeing the returns that one would expect. It is the leader and their team, along with ambassadors of the project, who will be bold and take the steps necessary to make their way to change. The key to this is that major changes require an understanding of why the previous behavior was needed so that as those behaviors change there is less of a chance of falling back into old patterns because the necessity is crystal clear. Having a handle of the structure of an organization at the beginning of change and laying a path forward that is clear and concise ensure that the new overall structure makes sense and is profitable in returns as well as in the pride taken by the team leading the change.

Notes

1 H. Mintzberg, "Structure in 5's: A Synthesis of the Research on Organizational Design," *Management Science* 26, no. 3 (1980): 322–41.
2 Indeed Editorial Team, "10 Types of Organizational Structures for Business," *Indeed*, March 11, 2023, https://www.indeed.com/career-advice/career-development/types-of-organizational-structures.
3 Max Freedman, "Types of Organizational Structures to Consider for Your Business," *Business News Daily*, February 21, 2023, https://www.businessnewsdaily.com/15798-types-of-organizational-structures.html.
4 D. J. Teece, "Explicating Dynamic Capabilities: The Nature and Microfoundations of (Sustainable) Enterprise Performance," *Strategic Management Journal* 28, no. 1 (2007): 1319–50.
5 H. Chesbrough, "Business Model Innovation: It's Not Just About Technology Anymore," *Strategy & Leadership* 35, no. 6 (2007): 12–17.
6 Ericsson, "5 G by Ericsson," https://www.ericsson.com/en/5g.
7 Peter Vanham, "A Brief History of Globalization," Geo Economics, World Economic Forum, January 17, 2019, https://www.weforum.org/agenda/2019/01/how-globalization-4-0-fits-into-the-history-of-globalization/.
8 N. J. Foss and T. Saebi, "Fifteen Years of Research on Business Model Innovation: How Far Have We Come, and Where Should We Go?" *Journal of Management* 43, no. 1 (2016): 200–27.
9 R. Ziatdinov and J. Cilliers, "Generation Alpha: Understanding the Next Cohort of University Students," *European Journal of Contemporary Education* 10, no. 3 (2021): 783–89.
10 Marcy Farrell, "Data and Intuition: Good Decisions Need Both," Harvard Business Publishing Corporate Learning, January 6, 2023, https://www.harvardbusiness.org/data-and-intuition-good-decisions-need-both/.

Chapter 7

Resources

The sixth theme to take into consideration is resources and how they are utilized. It can sometimes be the case that companies come too close to the day-to-day operations so that a mentality occurs of "this is how things are done." However, in stepping back to look at what a company has in resources and assets, it becomes possible to determine new exciting ways to deploy those strengths to grow and improve a business model.

Conduct a thorough review of key resources

Global development has enabled freer trade and increased resource use between countries. Nations have gone from being largely self-sufficient to creating international flows of products and services, which has also meant an increased focus on import and export issues.[1] The driving forces have been dominated by improved transport opportunities; increased travel, communication, and access to information; and the expansion of multinational companies. Resource usage is dependent on how well interdependencies and complementary pieces actually work together throughout the business solution.[2] It has become easier to access products and services from all over the world in everything, including food, clothing, household goods, music, cars, capital, travel, and much more. For companies, the focus can primarily be about driving the development of resources to find what is dynamic, but for international companies it is critical to find alternative products to create an even better solution because they are more exposed to rapid changes in the world around them. The companies that are at the forefront conduct ongoing reviews of their resources in order for the business model to be competitive in the same way that the best cars in Formula One are developed with the best available materials to ensure durability, reduce risks, increase speed, and be able to compete at the top.

The most common changes in a business model are a new activity in the chain, changing the composition of the chain, changing one or more partners, or creating a dependency between the parties that benefits from

DOI: 10.4324/9781003402121-7

both of them being in the model. When internal and/or external driving forces affect the structure in any of the previously mentioned ways, it is more often than not a case of a resource that is needed because it is lacking, missing right now, or may never have existed. For a company that is growing, resources are something that are more or less needed all the time. Resources can be a force that creates levers but also turns into padlocks if it is not made visible and taken care of well. Therefore, companies should make entire inventories of the most critical resources on an ongoing basis and have it as an active part of their annual business planning. There is a constant need for development of resources within a business model, especially when it reacts to external drivers.[3] This is time-consuming time the first time, then it is a matter of doing regular checks.

A new development in recent years is that a variety of different platforms connects with customers and then diversifies to create profits for those who are involved in creating offers. Technological development has also created different needs for natural resources and contributed to countries that have had a large supply of a variety of desirable resources becoming richer as a result.

For a company, it is about different types of resources to create growth in a good business model and be able to compete going forward. It deals with four main areas of resources: physical, organizational, human, and capital. We map between five and ten resources within these areas and assess, classify, and prioritize them accordingly. This is done early in the project and sometimes simpler improvements are already made here in the existing business model. This then serves as an important point of input both for the research methods used in the change project and later for subsequent seminars that gather opportunities and build a change agenda. In several situations, it has been absolutely crucial to know what resources are available, which ones will be required in greater volumes and which ones are missing to accelerate the growth in the new business model.

The medium-sized company was part of a larger industrial group with a focus on technical services. The company's business model was focused on larger external projects but also as an internal consulting organization in their area of expertise. The resources had previously been one of the company's great strengths; they knew all the factories and facilities locally and regionally, they had the latest technical tools/systems, they had developed internal services that supported the structure/business, they had experienced employees with good reviews, the formal structure was well known and worked for both larger projects and they had strong inventory management.

In recent years, the resources had changed as the parent company began to buy simpler services on a larger scale. The new CEO had several positions in the parent company and was looking after business. Gradually, the company's resources had begun to thin out and the existing business ended up in crisis when management removed key resources that were essential to be able to deliver, including two controllers and its own finance function.

When the parent company got a new CEO, a business model innovation case was created that looked at what had happened in recent years and what the company's business would look like going forward in the best-case scenario. The project started with business meetings and a review of all resources, then a review of the existing business model and later an extensive qualitative customer study was performed. It was a successful and extensive project that took three years from start to finish, with implementation starting after one year.

For the innovation projects, it is an advantage if all resources are inventoried early when the driving forces begin to affect the business model and for the company to already be in the initial conversations of changing the model. We also recommend that resources are updated on an ongoing basis, preferably once a year and added as part of the medium and large companies' annual business planning even if they do not feel that the model has any bottlenecks. It is equally important to go through the resources and compare against the existing business model and the company's strategies. The resources will most likely be used, modified, or redistributed during an upcoming work, but here it is mainly to be able to analyze how it affects the business.

A business model covers large areas with resources to create customer value and the driving forces are what usually trigger a change and most often the organizational structure is what then takes care of the change. The HR can be how the company trains its employees to gain more knowledge, what the company's experiences look like among the employees, how the workforce is distributed within the company, what skills and experiences the management have, how they take care of personnel issues, and much more. In most larger companies, the use of HR begins right at the start of the hiring process as there are more facts that need to be acquired with interviews, fact-checking, contracts with work tasks, and later also a job description that is accurate and specific.

The large international company acquired a number of companies in recent years and merged them into one group to cover more segments and be able to compete better. They were able to use the international organizational structure to build up the business via a number of factories around Sweden. Even before the acquisitions, they had conducted surveys that showed that the market would develop positively in their areas, and, above all, they were positive about future growth.

However, uncertainty existed around the sales organization's division of labor and which physical products would be leaders in the upcoming transition. In addition, management had done extensive internal work already and showed that there was a lack of internal knowledge of the product portfolio; however, this was partially corrected after a cleaning up of the portfolio and various disposals. The first projects had taken more than a year and now the company wanted to analyze the other resources and in particular the need for products and how the sales organization would work.

It therefore carried out an initial review of the existing business model, all strategies, all resources and also looked for the key resources for success. After that, work continued on an extensive qualitative study in their own sales organization, product dealers, prescribing consultants and with various end-user groups. It was also supplemented by a comparison with another country in the group. The work led to a clarification of product groups, more channels for messages and a changed flora of products with a focus on advanced solutions. The entire work also changed inventory management, the logistics in the store saved large costs, and the new products contributed with consistently better margins.

We usually do a mapping of about five to ten resources per group of human, organizational, and physical factors and supplement with questions on finances, which mainly relate to margin improvements and possible cost savings. In this mapping exercise, we assess needs in four different classifications: quality, quantity, supply, and price. This is not the same work that takes place in a regular purchasing department or linked to orders/ warehouses but is used for an assessment of the business model.

In the past year, the company had won several large business contracts that required more resources, which were needed in a short period of time. They did an initial check and called a two-part management conference to go through the situation and make an overall plan to move forward with the delivery. The conference was planned in two parts, with brainstorming and planning at first and sketching action plans and implementation in the following part.

At the first conference, the CEO went through the various contracts and showed the total need for resources with the question of what the company could manage themselves, how they could collaborate, and who would be in the best position to handle future deliveries. These were mostly physical products and the CEO outlined them in different factories. It was a good meeting where about 20 people who were leaders around the country and internationally gathered.

The next meeting focused primarily on material availability, equipment, products, various factories, technological assets/constraints, and local knowledge, which were important since several foreign factories would produce parts and deliver these to a factory to use the pieces together, enlist capital needs, and release tied-up capital. The CEO emphasized that they already had predetermined dates for orders with clear payment instructions where the majority were at final approval, which would also require subcontractors to line up on equal terms. The company therefore tried to create flexibility and offer smaller orders as well as larger orders so that they could in turn buy in larger volumes and be able to offer longer payment terms with preferably a minimum 90 days up to 180 days. The conference was a success and the company managed to deliver several new innovations to its largest customers.

When the projects work with resources and at the same time focus on customer value, it is important to focus on the organizational aspect and try to get the structure to help support the project. A leader needs to be positive about what the systems and people can offer and it always looks a little different from company to company. Concept development is a creative process – from identifying triggers/driving forces to understanding and analyzing the structure to then creating the concepts with the resources. It is about focusing on collaboration, identifying key data and people, planning, controlling, and reviewing all internal and external reports that exist, including secondary data and at the same time putting the first thoughts on what a project could look like, what needs to be informed/communicated, and how the project should be implemented. It is all about finding the best solution to secure the outcome of the business model and show how this could be done in the most valuable way.

Insights for conducting a review of resources

1. Make an early inventory of all resources
2. Update resources on an ongoing basis (list once a year)
3. Go through the existing business model
4. Resources in four categories (human, capital, structure, and physical)
5. Use the structure for value creation (dominant resources)

Reinforce if there is anchoring with the strategy and the business model

Global trade has developed extensively, which has led to greater incomes, less poverty, and more productivity. This has been driven by increased trade between countries. After World War II came the golden age of capitalism, which was an effect of a conference in the United States (Bretton Woods) aimed at reducing trade barriers and working for freer capital flows. As a result, the economically strong countries in particular were able to increase their international business with the help and orchestration of the United States.[4] The world economy increased by large volumes until the early 1970s when, among other things, the oil crisis contributed to stagnation. At the same time, several countries developed more international trade during the 1970s, 1980s, and 1990s than before.[5] When the recession subsided, the world economy received a new boost from the IT revolution from the early 1990s, and this has flourished for almost two decades, as well as trade liberalizations with the WTO. Medium and large companies began to spread their productions across more countries as an effect of the fact that it was now more possible than before and the market became more geographical and also specialized, which also contributed to greater opportunities with business model innovation. After the financial crisis in 2008, the world market has grown at a slower pace of about 2 percent per year.

When the pandemic came in 2020, there was a rapid downward effect, but the recovery has been positive despite concerns in the world. In the larger perspective, the global market has developed in line with population, with technology and collaborations being made to stimulate trade. The new world order has been greatly affected in recent years with the aftermath of the pandemic, with world trade slowing down and the fact that the WTO is not as important as it has been in the past. Much of 2022 had been about security policy and geographical disputes between countries, while at the same time the world is trying to switch to more climate-smart and sustainable alternatives. Global associations are under pressure from conflicts over who should have more control in a world order. There are a number of forces that believe that climate change needs to be stopped, among other things, by reduced globalization, while others believe that global technological development cannot be stopped.[6]

Technological development, together with minor trade barriers, has created new ways of running companies and also contributed to looking beyond national borders. Trains were the earliest vehicles used in transporting goods and people in large numbers and later buses and cars have become a natural part of our everyday lives. It is difficult to predict what the world will look like in 25 years' time, but for medium and large companies it is important to develop and create value through their resources. Those who work with innovations in a world market need to follow and understand what is happening more closely than ever before as a local change can have a major impact on business with, for example, extra taxes, import restrictions, competence issues, or currency impact. For business model innovation projects, it is important that the purpose is clarified and that a review of available resources is matched to the existing business model and what existing strategies look like. Often this happens gradually as the content of the project becomes clearer and the demand for data increases in order to later be able to analyze, lay a plan, and implement.

The international company's business model was adapted with production lines in several countries and with specialization as a direct result. To solve production capacity for profitable product areas, the company also bought factories to support continued growth. The segments were gradually harmonized; there was an adaptation to the market locally, but at the same time approximately the same channel strategy was built to reach out to customers and the value creation was the same regardless of the market.

They would lead the technological development in their field and offer unique products at the right prices for the right customer. The company had bought a larger factory in Sweden as part of the overall strategy five years before and had intended to primarily use the company's platform. The group had tried to establish offices in Scandinavia on several occasions without success. The purchase of the factory had been a success in the short term, but gradually it created many unanswered questions on resources.

The board decided to conduct an inventory of resources in an internal qualitative study, which was later entrenched. This led to a change in working methods and a move of production to another country mainly because technological development was judged to be better and more focused in a different production line.

When companies make the inventory of their resources and are clear on what they look like, it is important to try to explain whether there is contact with the existing business model and any existing strategies. We have seen that it is often crucial for future decisions going forward. It may be that the inventory shows that there are five welders of whom two are fully qualified and three are apprentices but ten welders are needed in the current business. It could then be shown that there is an elaborate strategy together with a local high school in the city that will deliver certified welders within an agreed period of time. It may be that the company uses pellet fuel in their production and will switch to other materials, but there is an agreement that extends for another five years and new pellet fuels are on the way.

The physical products can be easier to see (e.g., a factory) and are usually more expensive to exchange in and out from the business model. The organizational resources can be about systems that already exist and work projects that have longer agreements or existing collaborations that are missing resources but are already agreed on for future delivery. HR can be difficult to understand if a leader is missing the experience, judgment, or loyalty to cope with the current or upcoming change. If there is an anchoring that is deeper in the existing business and previous strategies, these should also be evaluated at the same time.

A midsize company with over 150 employees needed to change its services because the customer requested a different type of delivery. That change in delivery would mean longer and more demanding days for employees, unless the entire delivery was rebuilt.

The company first conducted a customer study to get to know the needs more deeply and be able to assess how and if it was possible to offer the services within the old business model or if it had to be completely redesigned. After the study was completed, an inventory was made in the company regarding the physical products, the staff's competencies, and the organizational resources with a focus on structural systems and collaborations.

This led to an extensive system change and training in computer literacy for about 75 percent of all staffs. The company then carried out a reorganization of its business and strengthened it with the resources that already existed and with new systems for the products and product training after computer knowledge. Data maturity was very low initially, but with a positive leader, a good team, and external ambassadors, the new deal became a game changer.

If an inventory is made carefully and together with consideration of how they relate to the model and any existing strategies, it can create other conversations and lead to cost savings later. The organizational processes are often about how we can create better profits from faster reporting or get a customer to participate more in an ongoing process. An inventory of resources can be time-consuming because there are several questions that can be difficult to answer later, such as how we assess if a group of ten people becomes more successful after completing the training, in regard to the inventory showing the group and their level of education in connection with the inventory and whether they have crucial system knowledge that needs to be continuously developed.

The large company handled big volumes of services and at the same time made an assessment that the market would seek system solutions rather than the manual processes around which the company's services were primarily built. They didn't have a direct, acute competitive situation at the moment but there were several early indications that other companies were interested in their large business volumes.

Their business model targeted this segment but also provided other business opportunities as a result of their special knowledge and experience.

They started a series of one-to-one meetings to assess the company's skills, workforce loyalty, and the company's brand.

After six months, work continued on a larger study that developed knowledge about the existing business and later a study was also done that included the world around them. After another 12 months, a software development of a new system began to be able to perform the previous manual service in with systems instead.

A business model depends on being able to create value for the customer and in that process, it is important to understand how and what resources are important in the short and long terms. We see an advantage in creating deep knowledge, and preferably early on, about all resources used in the existing business and whether there is a relationship to existing strategies already. This exercise is necessary, even if it is done at a glance, and usually in the early business conversations where the customer starts thinking along these lines. We then do a simpler review when we go through the existing business model later in the project. We have this with us as we go into the study and later also as an active part when we conduct seminars to analyze and work out which projects should be included in the upcoming change of model. There are early gains, especially in margins and cost savings and these issues are alive at the start of a change.

Insights for reinforcing the resources

1. Create deep knowledge for potential cost savings
2. Search for contact with or within the existing business model
3. Search for physical resources (more expensive with more potential)
4. Make an inventory of the intangible assets (organizational)
5. Go through the HR (search for potential strengths)

Focus on hidden values

The customer groups are getting bigger and bigger, but also more mobile and in this there is a hidden value in making the business models work faster, as the international trends show.[7] Rapid changes in the world around us require faster changes than before for competition and survival. Of course, there are also niche areas of products that, in the wake of rapid development, can be both profitable and sustainable.

The digital structure and organization are something that the young, particularly Generations Z and Alpha, have as an obvious basis of values and the question is what it means looking into the future.[8] By having a work force that has grown up with more contact with AI and tools like ChatGPT, it will allow for greater analysis and be a driver for change as the pace of evolution within customer segments increases. Those who are used to the openness and quantity of data will be able to search it more efficiently to ensure that any information that is necessary for analysis will be more accurate, which can in turn lead to the ability to be more predictive and effective in producing what will generate the best outcomes. The market will continue to look at business models that can create value for many, have sustainable value, and search for products that have underlying value by understanding customer needs faster than others.

The development of technology over the past 30 years has continued to create innovations that have become successful products and services for a world market. Today, we see an increased focus on the fact that the past few years have mainly been characterized by data integration and security on the Internet as the number of users has increased. Right now, we are in an era that is affected by the new tools given to us by AI, automation in different parts of the workplace and markets, the hybrid and flexible work space and routines, and with a circular service logic that shakes up the old way of thinking about organizations. The next generation Internet of the free intelligence algorithm has recently been introduced in the form of ChatGPT over the past several years and this will certainly further impact our digital solutions even more. The development will continue and is important for the producer who best satisfies the consumer's needs.

In most innovation projects, there are questions around products that relate to market conditions, the time to market for a change, costs for development, the unique properties of the products, and how it relates to the business model. It has become more important to try to understand whether it is possible to bring forward the launch of products, especially as many of these are improvements on already-existing technologies. If it refers to new development projects that do not develop or improve value to the existing business model then they need to be managed in another way and not as a business model innovation project. These cases are rather startup-related cases and have a different focus and usually require more venture capital.

The large international company had long since found various niches in manufacturing as their specialty. They had production facilities all over the world and had been the subject of purchases several times, most recently in the previous few years. The different ownership groups had one thing in common in that they focused on the company's unique products, but competition increased rapidly. Their product was an addition to the automotive industry, which meant that industry gradually took over with original equipment manufacturers from other competing manufacturers.

Recently, the company was bought again by an international investor group who bought companies frequently and focused on the data

*available about the products, content, and of course the customer and
supplier ledger. In recent years, the company had understood the need
to continue to develop its product in order to offer it even more uniquely.*

*They believed that there were still underlying values for the product
to be offered to other interesting segments as well. They implemented
one-to-one meetings and in the present day are now opening up an innovation case for speeding up their business model regarding the development of the product and the upcoming commercialization.*

Most innovation projects have more interest in physical products, partly
because there are often large investments if it is to be developed, but also
because there may be underlying values that can mean quite large profits if they can be released faster. It can refer to different types of physical
equipment that can enable other management methods, such as card and
passage systems that have had a fairly large focus within different groups.
It can refer to various locking functions that have a wide impact. Tools are
available in most industrial areas and something that can be used in a value
chain. It can also concern different types of raw materials, construction of
buildings for different areas, factories, technologies, certain locations, or
simpler products with broad patents that protect the special technology
contained in the product.

Product development is essential regardless because it benefits both the
producer and the consumer. It can also be a special design that is protected
and gives great effect via the business model. Different industries have different entry barriers that protect segments from rapid changes, which can
be general protection via patents, trademarks, and designs. However, even
the legislation can hinder or help and look very different between countries.

*The larger company understood that their knowledge could be exposed
to competition and carried out a digitization of the knowledge into a
unique product, namely software. The whole product was designed,
separately developed, and covered a unique area.*

*They also had their very own working methodology with internal
work that was designed over time and the market had quickly welcomed
the product. The company started a one-to-one meeting routine early on
to review the innovation project and ensure the rights with driving forces
into other groups as well.*

*This meant that the product was protected, the name was trade-
marked in some areas, and there was a greater hope of continuing into
other areas. The project continued into other areas with further external
studies and customer meetings. Four years later, the launch was complete, sales had increased rapidly, and profits were already high.*

Focusing on hidden values can apply to all or part of the business model
but the effects of doing so can mean so much more. It is about nurturing

the brand to create value with the customer and it contributes to increased growth and profit. A brand can be protected but also contribute positively to increased attraction from investors, employees, and partners. It is possible to get exclusive rights to a brand and then license and sell the logo. This also applies to manufacturing processes in business models; they can be interesting for partners who get to be involved and scale in a deal for both growth and profits. The design can also be protected and it can be valuable to have exclusive rights and attract investors and to enter into sales and licensing agreements. There may be copyright for something that is created in audiovisual texts, images, and music.

Business ideas and models cannot be protected with patents or other rights but it is quite possible to create a trademark and fill it with values that are linked with the idea and then it can be protected as a trademark. There may also be a need sometimes to protect a business model, which is done with regulated employment and assignment agreements. By regulating what employees can and cannot receive when their employment ended, the company can prevent a potential spread of key parts of the business model. Excellence is often a competitive advantage, and internal manuals with descriptions of work processes are intellectual property that can be sold or licensed. This also applies to databases and customer registers.

The company's business model had been developed over many years by the current owners who had carried out a management buyout two years earlier of their previous employer. They had great ambitions with the operations with six different businesses that were included in the acquisition, which was placed in a limited company. The acquisition included inventory, names, processes, and customers and the owners had put considerable resources into ensuring a good direct buyout.

The ambition going forward was a tighter business model that would have its own design, methodology, and other positive changes for the customer groups. By offering a special methodology, they expanded the opportunities to search for customers outside the regular groups and it could contribute positively to a more sustainable approach to knowledge development.

The company invested in rebuilding the business model with new strategies through an internal study and employee conferences. The changes took two years and were successful. A solid growth was achieved with better profit development for everyone involved and therefore they also introduced a reward system for all employees on an annual basis.

We see two clear groups regarding product innovations: those leaders who see products as a costly administrative process and those who see the process as the engine of the entire flow of innovations. In our projects, there has been a slow positive development as it has become more clear which resources are referred to in a business model innovation process. The second experience regardless of the resources referred to in the change is that after projects are completed it is always about understanding, insights, and behaviors to be followed.

The broader perspective of owning resources in innovation projects creates a balance between the structure, people, and strategies. The different resources add another dimension to each of these areas, which in turn can promote positive growth. We can map out which resources are important, set a goal as to what these resources can achieve, and search for alternatives for other measurement. It is about increasing the common knowledge to be able to solve the issues around how resources connect with the overall business model and the strategies. All this is about creating and developing customer value in a better model that enables better competitive situations.

Insights for focusing on hidden values

1. Search for underlying values in physical products
2. Fill the trademark with value (potential to register)
3. Focus on unique product development (potential profit)
4. Understand that the design can be valuable
5. Search for intellectual property

The right knowledge building innovations

The world of work has changed with the advent of the Internet, globalized trade, and the opportunities to work more flexibly.[9] It will be more important than ever to understand the workers of tomorrow's expectations, attitudes, and what builds value for them. Traditional structures will change as business models capture needs with new opportunities to organize and develop resources. It's like a marathon in very hot weather where participants are given the option to run without shoes on a paved road but who choose shoes and fluids every two kilometers to keep the body running. Business model innovation is also a result of the fact that business has been able to develop at a furious pace and new innovations have been created on the assembly line and then laterally in technology development.

Innovations require time and the stronger international companies are therefore more actively looking for knowledge that can be adapted at the right time. At the same time, the need that is identified creates the innovation means a change in behavior in the creation of the model also contributes to how quickly a corrected business reaches the market. We see from today's projects that needs are increasing and education is important. For the projects, we use the research methods as required and then develop a common platform for the knowledge that needs to be changed or added, which also means that their business models need to cope with invisible changes before it is corrected. The new knowledge may be there in the company's employees but is thwarted due to behaviors that contain other values.

Technological developments have already changed the view of how we educate ourselves from early classrooms to going to university. The open knowledge with the Internet in the background has meant that people can access other people's experiences and insights more quickly. Personal choice has been made more accessible and is based on three starting points in learning: attitude, time, and ability. It is possible to conduct entire training sessions in front of a computer screen, learn languages, and, of course, train details in a production process. In these cases, the levels of education can differ and the training looks completely different between those who organize the trainings and those who will be going through them. One result of this is that the leader and their team that will implement the changes in the model need to become more careful, analyze surroundings, analyze behaviors, analyze patterns, and understand how the internal values will be affected by an implementation.[10] It probably hasn't been any harder than right now to understand what the future might hold and its implications.

The company's previously successful business model had gradually met the customer's needs less well and now the discrepancy increased further as the market changed faster. The drivers of the market had changed and it had created a change in behavior and their customers wanted to use the products more often, longer, and in a different way. In addition, customers had been given increased financial responsibility and this affected the willingness to offer more alternatives otherwise they risked reduced customer groups.

The large company decided to analyze itself using an extensive business model innovation project that was carried out over almost three years. It became a completely new concept that allowed for a different use where customers could influence parts of the product and add value according to their own product (within reasonable limits).

The company adapted the product and it later also became part of the entire offer, which meant that more customers/places could benefit from this exciting new opportunity. It also meant that the company also needed to adapt its business model/delivery model closer to the customer as these could affect the content. This project took another number of years but was very successful.

We have noticed that innovation is the engine of a change project for business model innovation and that it takes a very long time for companies to build in this engine so that they can control the speed themselves. Owners, boards, and management have a great task to assess whether customers' changing needs correspond to a corrected speed or change to a completely new engine.

The factors affecting resources and their composition will also contribute to the impact of innovation, speed, and how well a business innovation project will be successful in implementation or not. An entire innovation case in a medium and large company will have greater success if there is anchoring in the business with elaborate strategies where resources can actively contribute. It is also based on initial inventories of resources and how the existing business model is made, important considerations are made of how resources harmonize with structure and organization, whether the right skills exist, and whether there are ongoing evaluations against the milestones that the project set from the beginning.

> *The international company had successively pivoted from supplying certain products to its customers to becoming a full-service provider to an entire market segment. Things had gone well and the company had created solid growth with good margins for several years.*
>
> *Now there were new indications that the market segment would shrink and change character going forward. In some areas, it had already begun and there was concern about development being able to proceed quickly. The company's sales departments sounded the alarm about a major impact on the existing business and that something needed to be done, otherwise margins would disappear drastically. The company decided to conduct a qualitative study that included internal key employees, existing customers, potential customers, and some competitors.*
>
> *The conclusions were handled in several seminars and then a corrected concept was created. In order for the arguments to be made even more visible, another internal study was conducted with the most important sellers within the company who were allowed to comment on and influence the final product. The challenge was that the company had previously created two channels as a manufacturer, a distribution network with retailers and a direct concept to larger customers in the segment and to customers they considered not belonging to the segment. It had now been exposed to foreign competition in the open segment with larger customers, and competitors then used these prices in comparison and contacted end customers of the distributors.*

It is important to create an early understanding of how resources should be used with more support so that they often develop faster. It can apply to the development and training of employees; it can address organizational changes regarding cooperation/new links between partners and it can concern the area of use of a newly built factory. The innovative attitude of seeing opportunities in driving forces is very beneficial for planning, coordination, and follow-up.

Companies that dare to do more are more active in their resources and invest more in active learning and have more vibrant strategies linked to their systems and processes. We understand that companies have better opportunities to run safer innovation projects and that these companies also attract better employees. Today we know more about innovation and how a company can rebuild an existing company and modernize its solutions with entrepreneurship and create new opportunities. The great challenge for the innovators (internal entrepreneurs also known as intrapreneurship) is to win the trust of the internal company and be able to overcome any internal resistance by being bold and using better logic and being able to strengthen the behavioral changes with positive stories about what these will contribute to when they are implemented.

The large international company constantly shifted focus with its opportunities, but it still did not change the business model significantly. Instead, the focus helped to search more actively for potential resources that could contribute to an even better implementation for the model in the long run. The company felt that the structure, organization, and entire implementation of the deal was one thing, but resources were more about trimming the outcome and possibly being able to contribute to better margins and lower costs. The increased profit could then be invested in even better technical solutions for future customers.

The technical contribution was in a company with expert know-how that would strengthen potential business in selected parts. It was very often about understanding how selected resources could contribute more actively to the solution going forward. The company's challenge was to gain access to these projects because customers, internal deliveries, and external deliveries often came too late.

They decided to implement one-to-one meetings to develop better strategies and possibly a corrected business solution. In the next step, they chose to conduct internal conferences in order to gather the knowledge of about 100 employees and be able to target their offerings. It contributed to a more modern business with more partners.

The best innovations are created in companies that invest more time and build more active knowledge by using intrapreneurship and anticipating how these unique solutions will contribute more actively. It is important to see that leaders also influence the implementation spirit actively by helping articulate the visions of the ideas and what they should contribute to, appointing and working through a good team and then having good ambassadors for the changes to be implemented. The best leaders of the projects are those who can create sustainable structures that help the innovations move forward and offer organizations that communicate where the creation of values is built into their upcoming solutions. For medium-sized companies, it should be synonymous with the CEO and where more large-scale companies exist, there should be driving forces created in a business development unit called business creation. A function is needed that has taken care of the value, analysis, and implementation of the company in a more active way than before.

Insights for building innovations

1. Innovation is the engine for change and creating a plan for control
2. Early understanding of resources develops faster
3. Invest more time in resources and get quicker return
4. The intrapreneurs need to win the internal trust
5. Invest more time and build more active knowledge

The importance of resources in implementation

Markets are changing faster in line with globalization and to understand these changes requires knowledge that, at the same time, takes longer to learn. There is also a cultural aspect to learning where we create groups of peers early on in our lives and gradually we get the opportunity to choose our own direction through post-secondary education and beyond. We can travel long distances in a short time to conduct business meetings; we have the opportunity to choose freer jobs but we still need to work to get our own livelihood. The major driving forces in society create new needs, new opportunities, and oftentimes very few win while others risk losing.

Part of this puzzle is control of the structures; another piece is the organization that enables better solutions and an important part is what resources are available to create solutions. At the management level, resource is often equated with capital, but in a market, it is very much about needs and what is possible to offer/implement. Today's leaders need to have more contact with themselves, dare more with others, and at the same time have insight into their losses and misses. Most business leaders have had losses during their careers and gradually understood that knowledge can be built on, and at the next loss, they do not sink as deeply. This allows them to be more robust, weather more storms, and eventually be able to preempt and avoid similar mistakes in the future.

Success is to also daring to lose in an implementation and not to get stuck in the resistance that comes but to listen and make the corrections that the project needs. At the same time, it is important to keep the momentum and the right direction moving and not act on the actions of others if the project's purpose is to steer in a different direction. For business model innovation projects, it is about leading through others, having a clear and realistic roadmap for the implementation, a resource description that relates to the business model and the strategies and to have a longer plan. Last, owners, boards, and management have a collective responsibility for all business models, concept development, and how the companies develop over time.[11]

The company had previously purchased a number of different resources to put together a concept where they could build their own unique solutions for industrial processes and industrial manufacturing. Since the beginning, the development had gone well and the units were gradually converted into production and there were still unique clients left in each area. They focused on one segment and the customer was close even though both the company and the customer were parts of large international groups.

Growth continued, the customer bought more, and the company employed many people while the business had constant needs. This led to several bottlenecks, and in order to cope with the customer's increased demand, a series of one-to-one meetings were carried out, and a model review existed in the form of a pilot study, a qualitative study, and five subsequent management seminars. It created a joint plan for a business model innovation with five projects that included 30 unique improvement projects.

The implementation was outsourced for one year and the entire company's staff was allowed to participate in small and large ways. The changes were closely followed and after another year, another study was conducted with five seminars to strengthen the company's entire spine using Three-Step Management. After three years, the company had increased its turnover by 150 percent and the results from the implementation were also positively noticeable on the income statement. During the implementation, the company chose to work closer to the customer and distribute the work to more international units. This reduced the risks for the company and meant that the specialization could go faster where previously it had not been possible to hire the right skills at high speed. For the customer, this meant that value creation was ensured, which also led to additional orders and increased relationship exchanges in more places in the world.

An implementation is dependent on the project being anchored and having a clear purpose. It is not certain that all the issues that emerge at the five to six management seminars will be implemented without an innovation case being sketched together and to ensure that it will later also be anchored with the management. We have noted that the companies with the greatest success have a detailed description but at the same time allow several activities to be handled by decentralized processes and only a few are centralized. The best companies also correct their plans and give themselves more time, even when there is a rush. Often there is a logic in the planning that can be used on overall issues, quality improvements, documentation, central resource issues, and purchasing issues/inventory, which includes a reduction of article registers, recruitments, collaborations with new partners abroad, and major changes in the model including changes from localities to regions, recruitments, or training programs. The list of different initiatives is very dependent on the driving forces, resources, strategies, and the already-existing business model. There is no list that says that these points must be included but they are very unique from project to project.

> *The large international company received many orders within the current business model and initially made an assessment that changes would be required. They convened two joint conferences and there they succeeded in planning, developing a model for implementation, and later also taking decisions.*
>
> *They solved the implementation by rescheduling large parts of the resources that would be required and dividing the purchases into smaller and larger deliveries. It created a better flow of capital but also ensured that they could distribute the purchases better and use more production facilities around the world that could produce on a smaller and larger scale.*
>
> *The increased logistics were a calculated risk that was later added to the mutual contracts with both the customer and the subcontractors. Most partners were known in the network, but some were new to the recommendations. There was internal resistance to this solution because the deliveries required increased collaborations, more time, and more customer explanations.*

A business model innovation project benefits from having a clear way of working to map out which parts need to be improved and later implemented. We have been very permissive to successive improvements in initial reviews of existing models but gradually also informed the leader about the risks of implementing changes that are not anchored. If it intends to redistribute labor resources between countries, the company requires quite extensive measures that also include local negotiations with unions and perhaps other centralized issues, which take more time. Larger companies are more accustomed to scaling their processes and often have resources allocated to project implementation, but we believe that these projects also require more from the leader, team, and ambassadors – they must have an overall understanding, decision mandate, and must be able to listen to and answer questions.

The existing business needed to change and therefore the company had made a customer study and various initial adjustments. Their main product was an information system that had been sold internationally to different segments in closely related industries and the study gave them important answers as to how to change their future offer.

Therefore, the work resulted in new modules and some potential new segments within the same industry but also outside in other industries as well. The challenge lay in future implementations, communication, and marketing. The implementation was done through user meetings, new descriptions, communication in several channels, and invitations to a number of conferences where potential customers had been hand-picked to attend.

The company received the selection of potential customers from the user meetings, their own search, and help from experts in digital marketing. Two years later, the company had established itself in a large new country and had more customers in more segments.

With so many resources at different levels of a company, having a handle on the importance of the entire inventory at a company is an essential part of understanding the business and is a crucial part of improving and changing a business model. In understanding how resources are distributed and their utility throughout the production process, it allows leadership to be able to more accurate in identifying and getting ahead of where these resources may be under/overused or how to better distribute them to create overall efficiency. In allowing others the opportunity to lead and in being bold enough to try new things and learn from the wins and losses, leadership can find the most effective use of all the resources at their disposal to compete in an ever-changing market while also ensuring value and customer satisfaction from order all the way through to delivery.

There have been many short descriptions of different issues, how different companies handled the driving forces, and the results of different implementation. The single most important issues for success are that there is a leadership that works through others using Three-Step Management, a clear and realistic action plan, resource description that relates to the business model and strategies, a longer plan which describes what the effects will land later, and a plan for communication with reconciliation points and reversal where needed.

Insights for understanding the importance for resources

1. Leadership that works through others (Three-Step Management)
2. Identify the clear way forward, which parts need to be improved and later implemented
3. Anchored and having a clear purpose
4. Detailed description but few are centralized
5. Be bold and allocate time and resources

Summary

It is often easy to underestimate how important it is to consider all the resources available when undergoing a change project. While it may seem an obvious thing to look at, resource management can sometimes be left to one side while strategy and processes are elevated. When undertaking a business innovation case, it is crucial to have resources inventoried early rather than late, particularly when driving forces begin to affect the business model. Once that initial list is made, it must be updated on an ongoing basis, ideally once a year, and added as part of the annual business planning in medium and large companies. When going through the Three-Step Management model, Step Two is where resources are considered, and this is the time when they are compared against the existing business model and strategies. In taking stock of the resources available, it helps to map them in the categories of human, organizational, and physical resources and consider the questions around finances, particularly in the classifications of quality, quantity, supply, and price. When resources are dominant and focused on customer value, it helps to get the structure to reinforce the project.

When an inventory is carefully made of all the resources available and considered with how they relate to the model and existing strategies, it creates other conversations and cost savings later down the line as deep knowledge is created. In taking time to have a comprehensive inventory of resources, all resources become visible which illuminates where there is contact with the business model and strategies, which is a critical part of the process, and it is important to complete this step in its entirety. Through this process, the physical products are easier to see and tend to be more expensive to change in and out of the business model while the organizational resources are about the systems that already exist and are working. These resources often have longer agreements and when considered carefully they can shed light on the collaborations that are missing. The HR rely heavily on the understanding of the leader; if the leader does not have the required experience, judgment, or loyalty, it can be difficult to understand or cope with the current state of HR or upcoming changes through the change process. While it may be time-consuming to create a fully comprehensive view of the resources in a company, it can do nothing but be of use to create a foundation for lasting positive change.

As a change project progresses it can be an exciting thing to discover hidden values that have been buried within an existing business model. Sometimes there may be more interest in physical products or large investments but as resources are developed it can come to light that there are underlying values that were previously unseen. This comes from owning resources in innovation projects, which creates a balance between structure, people, and strategies. It is important to understand that business ideas and models cannot be protected by patents or other rights; however, it is possible to create trademarks that are then developed by the ideas, which then lends protection. Even so, product development is essential because it benefits the consumer and producer by focusing to create value with the customer, which in turn increases growth and profits. This means that it is valuable to develop designs that can be protected as exclusive rights as this attracts investors and provides leverage to enter into sales and licensing agreements. Above all, excellence is a competitive advantage. By developing intellectual property, including internal manuals with descriptions of work, it creates an avenue to sell or license these properties. There are two clear groups that would find this of value – leaders who see products as a costly administrative process and those who see the process as the engine of innovation. In finding ways to create value both inside and outside an organization, it can provide whole new ways of considering a company.

When going through a change project, it is critical to find a way to build innovations throughout the process. Innovation is the engine of change in business model innovation. In some cases, it can take a very long time to build this engine to allow management to be able to control the speed themselves. When considering innovation and pairing this with the factors that affect resources and their composition, it can impact the speed of development and how successful a project will be in innovation. Where there is an understanding of how resources should be used, innovation often develops better. Those companies that dare to do more, are more active in their resource allocation, and invest in active learning will develop more vibrant strategies that will be linked to systems and processes. The greatest challenge for those who innovate within a company (intrapreneurship) is to gain the trust of the internal company. What is clear is that the best innovations are created in companies that invest more time and build active knowledge by using intrapreneurship and taking the time to anticipate how these unique solutions will contribute to the company in an active and dynamic way. It is not enough to change a business to generate success; a business must innovate and become dynamic.

The final piece of the puzzle is to successfully implement and sustain changes to the business model that will allow for growth and the flexibility to evolve when necessary. The most critical factors for success are that there is a leadership team who knows how to lead through others, that there is a clear and realistic action plan, that there is a resource description that relates to the business model and strategies that lay out a long-term plan addressing which effects will be active later as well as a plan for communication along the way that takes into account reconciliation/milestones and what to do in the case of reversal. It is a big thing to ask, but by taking time throughout a change process from beginning to the end, creating a strategy that takes into account these factors for success will save time and resources and push the company toward their goals more effectively.

Business model innovation projects always benefit from having a clear way to map out what parts of the business need to be improved and later allow plans to be implemented to make the necessary changes. The process of implementation must have strong anchors, including timelines and set goals as well as an overall purpose that is clear and understandable by all. Those companies who have seen the greatest success are the ones who have detailed descriptions of the change they want but allow several activities to be decentralized and only have a few that are centrally controlled. This means that plans can be pushed a little further even when there is a rush to see the changes made. While larger companies are more accustomed to having innovation projects ongoing in their organizations and have the resources allocated for project implementation, this does not always equate to success. They must also have an overall understanding, have a strong decision mandate, and be able to listen to and answer questions.

For some leaders, getting to grips with resources in the process of change is either the most exciting or the most daunting part of the process. It can be an enlightening thing to see what is at hand to innovate and create change, but in the same way, it is also frustrating to see what has been missed, especially in legacy companies. However, so long as a team going through a business model innovation project can do so with their eyes open and be willing to be bold in their strategies and resource management, then it is an adventure that can lead to great success and pride in all those willing to take the chance.

Notes

1 Peter Vanham, "A Brief History of Globalization," Geo Economics, World Economic Forum, January 17, 2019, https://www.weforum.org/agenda/2019/01/how-globalization-4-0-fits-into-the-history-of-globalization/.
2 C. Zott and R. Amit, "Business Model Design: An Active System Perspective," Long Range Planning 43, no. 2–3 (2010): 216–26.

3 T. Saebi, L. Lien, & N. J. Foss, "What Drives Business Model Adaptation? The Impact of Opportunities, Threats and Strategic Orientation," *Long Range Planning* 50, no. 5 (2017): 567–81.
4 M. Wolf, "Shaping Globalization," *Finance & Development* 51, no. 3 (2014): 22–25.
5 Ibid.
6 Vanham, "A Brief History of Globalization."
7 H. Chesbrough, "Business Model Innovation: It's Not Just About Technology Anymore," *Strategy & Leadership* 35, no. 6 (2007): 12–17.
8 Renee Hanlont, "You've Heard of Millennials and Gen Z, but What Is 'Generation Alpha,' Exactly?" *Parade.com*, April 6, 2023, https://parade.com/living/generation-alpha.
9 Kevin Webb, "From the Internet to the iPhone, Here Are the 20 Most Important Inventions of the Last 30 Years," *Insider*, May 17, 2019, https://www.businessinsider.com/most-important-inventions-of-last-30-years-internet-iphone-netflix-facebook-google-2019-5?op=1&r=US&IR=T.
10 Marcy Farrell, "Data and Intuition: Good Decisions Need Both," Harvard Business Publishing Corporate Learning, January 6, 2023, https://www.harvardbusiness.org/data-and-intuition-good-decisions-need-both/.
11 Dominique Turpin, "Top Leadership Qualities in Today' s Unpredictable World," IMD, April 2016, https://www.imd.org/research-knowledge/articles/top-leadership-qualities-in-todays-unpredictable-world/.

Chapter 8

Summary

Deeper explanations of factors to conduct a successful business model innovation and how it really works

In this book, I have presented six different themes and 30 success factors, which culminate in 150 insights. The ideas can work well as a starting point for companies that need to develop their existing business model and analyze which factors can more safely contribute to a better process and more profitable growth. The framework increases the opportunities for analyzing the business model, understanding driving forces, seeing different connections in that business model, clarifying bottlenecks, and being able to develop a good basis for safer implementation.

The journey of innovation usually begins with initial meetings between me and the customer to discuss and set a clear objective. In the smaller projects, it can be two or three meetings, and in the larger ones, there can be significantly more as we analyze a variety of facts about the business. Once we have agreed on a collaboration and have generated an opinion of what needs to be done, we take time to itemize and understand the existing business model in the second step. In this initial work, the framework has a reconciliation function where we can talk our way through the different functions of the company, including: segment, customer, relationships, value, the different communication channels, key resources, the structure, the organization, margins/costs, and deliveries. I recommend this step because here we can make short and rapid improvements to the business model where we see obvious shortcomings that may not have had time to grow into full bottlenecks. It is usually appreciated that this time is taken to work and go through clarifying the model and talk about the price/value of what the company creates. In this process, the concept can be the wind that sets off in the boat's sails again and steers further toward expected destinations.

DOI: 10.4324/9781003402121-8

After that, most of the projects continue with in-depth studies, quantitative surveys, qualitative interviews, a mix quantitative and qualitative work, and focus groups. As the company moves forward with in-depth understanding, the six themes can serve as keys when it is indicated that it is necessary to go for deeper understanding. The initial conversations, objectives, and review of the existing model often form the basis of an interview guide and a foundation for the data to be collected.

The company conducts interviews according to an interview guide and encodes the results against the main headings and subheadings by building quotes and then they can make compilations and analyze the outcome in the different factors themselves. The framework can also be used directly as a mirror to the existing business model by building various seminars and focus groups. When the initial meetings have been completed, improvements in the business model have been addressed, and the company has conducted in-depth studies, the framework reflects the results back to the company when management conducts subsequent seminars with the reports as a baseline. In the initial meetings, I often brainstorm around what has emerged, which analysis points stand out, and how we could change the company's customer deliveries. These meetings aim at a plan to implement and improve the existing business model and the framework can act as a mapping within its six themes, 30 success factors, and with 150 insights.

The scope of the GUIDE and ATLAS is extensive. The various data points that are collected can be used for preventive purposes, as a response to

How it works

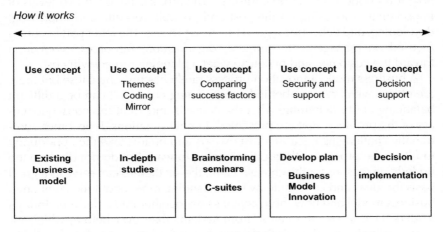

Figure 8.1 A perspective on how Business Model Innovation really works.

needs caused by bottlenecks, or to assist the company that wants to grow and tries to get an idea of how the future use of resources will affect customer deliveries.

The roles of the GUIDE and the ATLAS are: (1) help to view an objective; (2) review and understand the existing business model; (3) analyze against conducted interviews; (4) ensure the development of a plan for implementation; and (5) to have as a mirror for training later where the company's own strengths are highlighted. It will simplify the purpose and be able to focus more on customer value while strengthening the strategies for the business model.

The importance of the six themes for creation of business model innovation

The direction of the business model and how the strategies should help with an integrated set of activities in order to compete better are ongoing issues and are often the very premises for initiating a change. In the initial meetings, the project needs to focus on the possibilities of the existing business' strategies to understand how they are integrated and whether they are cohesive in order for customers to be prepared to pay the rates that will sustain the business. The starting point is that customers cannot be controlled, but the company has an idea of why customers purchase from them and has chosen segments and later also started to deliver how they will reach the potential customers. The whole framework has been possible in the past because it was about focusing solely on an existing business model and now it is about what can be improved. The projects have the two levels of importance in focusing on the cost and possible revenue and improving, developing, and delivering a good business process. The latter part becomes focused on management, structure, organization, resources, orientation toward the customer, and of course what a planning project will cost.

A business model innovation process rarely has just one cause but there are often several reasons behind an upcoming change. It can be a difficult balancing act to determine what the cause is and what the consequences are of the problems that are presented. In new situations, it becomes additionally challenging because most owners and boards take the opportunity to fill up the process with questions going forward but do not disclose the underlying reasons for the change. Here, the six themes can serve as a good basis for ideas and contribute by understanding more about the company's business model and how these activities tie together into a delivery. Today's leaders have more information from systems than ever before, which for some can help speed up their decisions, but for others it means that additional facts are needed to be able to make their decisions. The increased amounts of data can be interpreted in one way by some companies and by others in a completely different way. A major challenge is that leaders today need to select a lot of information from different sources and then make their own decisions.

Expectations are also linked to available time and today it takes a lot of planning to be able to implement changes. Questions and models have the advantages to be able to build plans before a change project happens or at best as part of something as it happens. More and more homework will be needed for leaders which is a relatively new phenomenon for most people. In order to accommodate a change at all, it is essential that a comprehensive message is anchored and it usually starts with actual problems or new opportunities. The message will first be investigated and then funded before finally being communicated through implementation. It takes more of leaders today to keep the strategies focused and at the same time to be able to marshal the company's resources more directly. It is challenging to be a leader and live with high expectations in medium and large companies. To succeed, companies need good business models that develop customer needs and strengthen long-term relationships. Decision-making is different where management is more dependent on quick information, communication, and that the company's brand is not only the product sold in a store but needs to be packaged more with invisible values.

This book can help in future transitions where the systems are gradually adapted and more of the decisions can be authorized further down the organization. The map can work as a guideline from the themes as they connect to the business model, which opens to all of the factors while introducing insights that will help to secure the transition and make the process more profitable. It is not a process model; it's not an analysis tool; it's not giving answers to every question for a medium or large company, but it is very useful as a concept in the creation of values in a change in an existing business model chain. The framework presents six themes that my customers have developed in my company over time and 30 factors that will help a business innovation project become easier and more successful. The factors include a combination of questions, inventory suggestions, and statements in 150 insights. Overall, the framework includes many different approaches; it is not meant to solve all questions in business model innovation but it can act as a safety valve in a way that is sometimes used by quiz shows, where you can call a good friend to help you, you can use the entire audience through voting, or you get two instead of four alternates to choose from. The ideas can offer a gradual deepening from its developed themes, the different success factors and, if you want to go really deep into the model, develop from the insights.

The different success factors are of different importance for each project and in subsequent implementation. They have jointly functioned cohesively for the different strategies and simplified the companies' planned implementation. Some of the success factors have been more central than others for the implementation of business model innovation and as an active part of my own work as an action researcher. For the initial discussions about strategy and customer value, living strategies have been and are something that has developed more possibilities along with being focused on simplifying and ensuring that the strategies carry something to the customer of value. After that, it is very much an attitude when reviewing the business model and how it is aimed at the customer and whether the model has an anchored process.

A great advantage over time has been the use of the Three-Step Management model as a methodology for change, which creates clear expectations for those who will gather facts, set boundaries, are involved in creating new data, make the process visible, develop a plan and later will also be involved in an implementation of what the company says it is happy with to proceed. It is also not possible to ignore all the variables that affect change and what I call variables for speed in the organizational structure. It is usually the variables that determine how quickly the organization can manage its development as customer orders increase. In an innovation process, it is therefore important to include all three perspectives and solve the structural perplexity – the variables, the human aspect, and the strategic elements. Since a business model can also be built in many different ways, it is good to try to decide how it should be assessed and what driving forces influenced these three horizons. Most larger companies measure effects and build reports, but when reviewing structural perplexity by weighing more perspectives, analyses often show that measurement rather reduces flexibility.

Last, I also need to highlight planning and follow-up in customer relationships. The best companies are proactive, work very closely with their customers, have a good idea of current needs, plan consistently, have regular contacts, and have ongoing feedback from planned follow-ups. I ensure that I have this with me when we set up the projects as a model for the companies I work with.

How to manage the process of business model innovation

Most companies have their own unique way of creating and setting up their business model. I have observed that there are still great similarities between the companies and how the value chain works much the same, regardless of the scale of the project. It is important to spend a lot of time at the beginning of an innovation project to understand how the model creates value, which strategies support the model, how the entire chain works, and which margins affect profitability. Of course, it is also important to get an overview of what driving forces are interfering with the existing model, the company's own perception of its key resources, and whether there are any known visible bottlenecks.

Strategy

For the business model, the traditional view is that strategy focuses on why and how value is created and what customers will then buy from the company. It is about understanding the holistic perspective from the industry and how the company should position itself to create unique value for its customer. It's less about being the best and winning but more about how companies are going to find unique value for their customer in a market. It is typically expected that customers cannot be challenged but the company wants to reach them through its strategies, which need to be coherent and clear. Of course, it is also about the existing customers, but the point of departure is still that they cannot be controlled, but with a better mindset and idea, it is possible to compete better.

The big difference for the company undergoing business model innovation is that the project later also includes planning and it takes care of the costs of what the strategies create for the company's customers. Strategy has two major functions for value creation in the business model: to either create value directly with the price that the customer is willing to pay or through the employees who contribute to a decrease in profits for them but an increase in value for the company. Of course, this may mean that the company is looking to deliver better but it is still about higher price or lower cost with deliveries that are well done. It is above all about the best projects where there is harmony in the messages, well-being, and a focus on knowledge. A change in a business model affected by increasing winds that are about to blow up into storms needs to pick up the pace to seek shelter and wait for better weather. If the business model has been damaged by the storm, it will have to replace broken parts, be repaired in detail, be tested, and increase the pace again when the wind has died down.

To ensure its implementation, it is crucial to clarify the functioning of the strategies of the existing model through an inventory. It is primarily about understanding the conditions for the project and whether it is possible to trim certain strategies directly via price corrections. The initial improvement can be an important part of a project financing where there is a need that can add value while the company can continue to work on what needs to be mapped and improved in general, usually the more extensive bottlenecks or repairs. It is equally important for creation to understand the working conditions of the staff and how they view their efforts at work, at home, and in their free time. The strategies can help create an advantage that can be improved or trimmed.

When I work with review of strategies, I try to create more space for my customer to be able to take time in refining, evaluating, and planning future strategies. There can be conflicting feelings in management on creating more time because many projects have direct needs with a business model that changes in unpredictable ways, doesn't work well, or sometimes doesn't work at all. In those situations, the early improvements to the existing business model are a way to create more time or to carry out a shorter pilot study that can help more directly. When it comes to more radical changes, the strategies need to be shifted, and it is important to find the best possible way to create new strategies for value development. The entire work needs to be done in agreement between the various decision-makers in order for it to give the best results, that is, between owners, the board, and management. Due to the development of communication, employees have become closer to management, which in itself means that the leader needs to have more self-control. If there is not enough time, there is a great risk that the strategy process will not be thought out or that the work will be affected by old attitudes of management. The leader needs to understand their own reactions and ensure that the focus is on leading through others.

The corrected or new strategies should be short, clear, and logical in order to be able to understand them more easily. I usually allow the leader and the team to test writing out long strategy descriptions, five to ten lines at most, and then choose a few words that will carry half of the text. It is important for understanding that the group itself is involved in developing the reasoning about the value and strategies. The strategies should also have a good beginning, a clear end, and be possible to communicate to justify the change in value creation. When I carry out brainstorming activities, it is extra important to create a good start to the meeting and put effort into ending positively. I do this by offering individuals and groups to create visible results and deliver different ideas in possible projects. Several projects have also shown that those very strategies that have the clarity with a good start and a clear end are the ones that lead the changes and give the best development of the process and the results.

The understanding should be built on the fact that the company stands for its values and that there is a common responsibility, which can be measured. The measurement is primarily aimed at being able to develop, simplify, and follow goals more easily. When the companies are bigger, they also become more dependent on everyone involved moving in step to be able to develop processes in the same way as it feels when cruising on a highway. There is nothing better than the feeling of all the parts of the machinery working with the driver to get to the desired destination, especially when the road is clear and the weather is fine. The achievements can be about the individual but, above all, it is grounded in groups and the company. The overall starting point is that the strategies normally should simplify for the business model and structure to create and deliver value to the customer but it is mostly a balancing act of many internal and external questions to consider.

The strategies are reinforced if they can discern surroundings, behaviors, patterns, and opinions and can be loaded with values. There is a story that describes how the queues meander outside the bread shop on a hot summer day. Several people crowd ahead in the long queue as they happen to do on an ongoing basis with people when they see a crowd ahead, but when our leader comes, they stand at the end of the line and wait for their turn. They stand there smiling as they chat with people before them in line and gradually people stop crowding. The leader uses their energy and body language and is motivated. They are also empathetic, which is an important characteristic. The strategies should be caring, leading, and able to be communicated with a clear vision. For the existing business model's actors, partners, and possibly others involved, there also needs to be something about efficiency that allows the model to keep the momentum going and perform the work that adds value.

The large companies often have a more complicated structure, more people involved, and there can be demanding processes to be able to deliver customer value. In these cases, the strategies should be alive – living strategies – to capture attention, which highlight and reinforce a company. Most major projects have resistance in behaviors and it takes more to stimulate or clarify. It can be stories that are close to the customer and describe in more detail what happens in the change at different stages. It can also be examples directly from the customer who comes in and helps to make it visible that there are people involved with the customers. They should be very close to the customer and be able to describe their daily activities. The strategies need to be tighter, more focused, and be more clearly prioritized. It can be the schedule that is made additionally concise for the entire process, it can be the quality that is tightened, or it can be special moments in the value creation that are shortened or that the company chooses to staff with fewer employees who are more skilled and therefore can more easily prioritize according to their experiences. In the implementation, it is often a central moment that companies get the behavior to click in through a team that teaches the next team and then the pace increases. It should be easy to explain a living strategy, and it can also be used for proximity and energy between different generations and in diversified companies that need the support of a clear direction.

Existing business model

The business model should basically create, develop, and manage customer value. It is important to have ongoing reconciliations to continue to develop knowledge about what creates customer value. It is important to create a structure that can recognize ignorance and where understanding is lacking early on in order to deliver. When a project starts, the leader and team need to review and identify early agreements for the existing business model. They need to ensure that they have full access to a complete set of facts and understand which behaviors are central for the model to be value-creating for customers.

Time is needed to carry out an evaluation of the business model and understand what works well and less well. Better companies continuously focus on internal reviews of collaborations, bottlenecks, and which strategies are important for value. They measure the development of customer value and link it to deliveries of services and products. It is a creative process to investigate the business model where management needs to enable the conditions with time and questions. At the same time, leaders need to be active listeners and show consideration for the answers that come from within the organization, from partners, or directly from customer-oriented relationships. A good review of the existing business model requires planning, mapping, and time.

An implementation of an evaluation of how customer value is created today needs to be anchored at all levels from owners, the board, and management. It is often a social process to create the bridges between the different levels of decision-makers that require time and space. The company's opportunities are in everyone's interest, but there is always a risk that some groups have more insight and access to facts than other groups and this creates an imbalance in decision-making. It is important to work to ensure that all decisions can be trusted and supported with relevant facts. There needs to be an agreement in the company's business model as to what should be included in a decision-making situation, particularly how the decision should be made, and who gets to make it.

I have seen a trend in recent years that medium and large companies are happy to empower selected individuals and move on from those decisions that in turn mean that the people have ordered without documentation, wrong volumes, wrong quality, or any other reason that contributed to a major bottleneck. For the projects, it is a matter of trying to understand the underlying causes and later make the necessary corrections. There should be insight into current customer value and how it is created at all levels from top management down to local units in international companies.

The best companies spend more resources on understanding their customers' behaviors that lead to purchases. Through an in-depth effort that clarifies and explains how customers act, they can develop a better process for their business model. It can be about qualitative interviews, surveys, focus groups, or trying to understand attributes via data orders. They look for unique values that protect the company's competitiveness and often build in specific resources that also make it difficult to copy. It can be some technical self-made details that the customer's entire solution depends on which from the outside may look easy to copy, but on the inside there are resources that cannot be produced by anyone else. In addition, if there is an extra value for customers together with a production chain that works, it is a strong competitive protection. The better companies continuously follow up and evaluate customers' perceptions of collaboration ability, quality, and deliveries. Through various types of inventories, tests, and future projections, companies get a better idea that the pricing is right and where it may go in the future. The value is what the customer is prepared to pay and from this value the company creates its business model.

The internal and external communications are variables for growth and harmonizing human behaviors. Companies need to clarify how they work with their communication and which channels will strengthen what areas. A communicative inventory needs to be made together with the review of how the strategies will strengthen the value of the best business solution. In the communicative review, the starting point is again the customer's value and how communication can help create the best possible conditions for a good customer delivery. It also needs to help create images of what the follow-up processes should look like and how the company can make early shortcomings visible. The best companies have their own plans for customer meetings, meeting content, joint seminars, on-call systems, complaint departments, and much more. There are great gains in understanding customers' buying behaviors to strengthen a long-term good solution for both parties.

Customer orientation

For the medium and large companies, it is important to follow the external drivers as this affects growth positively and negatively. They need to have an ongoing inventory of the most important issues that could possibly affect their conditions. It can be about environmental requirements, political changes, new technical solutions, upcoming quality labels, infrastructure issues, low-cost imports, smaller market due to increased competition, industry slippage, capital availability, changed product range, availability of labor, skills transfer, regulatory requirements, willingness to invest, and several other issues. They need to take an international stance if they operate in multiple markets against strong competition where change can happen more quickly. The better companies follow their customer groups closely, try to be at the forefront of trends, and identify and adapt values when needed.

There is a great advantage in having a management structure for customers that works proactively and follows the business closely, namely by having a customer manager. There is also a benefit in following customer value more closely and understanding how it can contribute to developing a better structure and organization. The most common way to develop a willingness to cooperate is to have regular follow-ups with seminars that include international supervisors and to sometimes invite experts who can show you the intangible assets. Customer orientation is about building relationships with the right customers, segments, and the partners who can contribute to the selected segments. It is fundamental to have a good and clear marketing strategy based on the existing business model. The new companies include more areas that also revolve around pricing strategies and revenue streams. They also have more activities around value-creating issues and what can contribute to new innovations in the long run.

By being active in the market, companies create competitive advantages, with increased awareness of needs, and also increase the opportunities to find customers who are prepared to test new purchases for alternative values. Today, customer groups are more sensitive due to the increased range of products, which also means that companies need to spend more time on their brands and fill them with soft values. A company is no longer just a product but also very much the company name, sustainability, quality, stories, good leadership, fair working conditions, opportunities to work flexibly, and much more. The younger generation of workers has completely different access to information and communicates on other platforms and the company needs to be consistent in everything it does. It can be additionally challenging when companies operate in several countries and have to adapt to trends, driving forces, and unique abilities within these different markets. It is important to be able to create value that can be understood by more people in the large organizations and to have clear value-creating policies that are followed by everyone. The multinationals' customers also have products and services in several countries, which put pressure on deliveries, regardless of where the companies produce.

It is important to have well-thought-out, detailed, and focused strategies that support the companies' business. It is essential when creating the customer-oriented solutions to see opportunities and think bigger without losing the sense of reality. It is more important today than before to understand customer behavior, be able to offer the right resources, and be prepared to contribute to more knowledge that develops the common value. The best companies are constantly working to improve their business solutions by being proactive and offering active support to their most important customers. When companies focus and prioritize value-creating activities, it can also mean that customers are provoked into action toward the organization rather than away from it.

A customer value is reflected in the price in terms of what the customer is prepared to pay and should not be overvalued or undervalued. If the company over-delivers, in practice it means that the margin will be smaller. What the company should deliver is the product that is in the agreement with all the quality and quantity expectations along with meeting delivery obligations. It is a complex issue to predetermine prices that both need relevant facts and are preferably supplemented with experience for all companies. The entire work with the business is simplified if the process is open, focused, and with straightforward communication. It is essential with the deliveries that there are descriptions for the entire chain of the business model in many ways. If it works, then there is an opportunity for world-class delivery.

Management

The technological developments of the past decade with increased accessibility to information have changed the conditions for management to control and lead companies. New leaders today are expected to look for tasks and to have greater insight and knowledge of the company already when they start a new assignment. At the same time, they will have to adapt their leadership style to the values of previous managers in their decisions, but good companies usually handle these issues more openly. Management needs to be familiar with the value creation of the business model and preferably have previous experience of the processes if they are not recruited internally or from the industry. The CEO should always be part of a change project of the existing business model and ensure that the anchoring is available to the board and owners. It simplifies things if the CEO is part of the group leading the change, and in the smaller medium-sized companies, it is not uncommon for them to be the leader in this model.

Management needs to stand behind all decisions to be implemented in a business model innovation project and harmonize messages, behaviors, and loyalties. They need to lead with examples and be clear that the project needs different amounts of time to raise the issues during early reviews and to analyze and influence the development of significant behaviors in the implementation. Management needs to help with understanding and identifying bottlenecks and behaviors, in that it has a well-thought-through, planned, and careful implementation. The help is primarily intended to contribute with explanatory strategic images that enable self-understanding among those involved in the projects and create creativity and better customer value. Success factors can be used as a mirror when the development seminars are conducted and therefore management can focus more on the content.

The new leadership with increased accessibility, more information, and more channels for communication affects and contributes to companies needing to offer a more open solution. For the CEO, this means that they need to be able to act in a more open environment where the person is more exposed to reactions than before and therefore also needs to understand themselves more. It is becoming more common for managers to increase transparency throughout the company with facts that have been centralized and previously only visible to C-suites. For the business model innovation project, it is central to get access to all the facts needed, whether it relates to customers, partners, employees, or anything else in the business model that contribute to value.

Management can also be a leader in adding new knowledge where needed and contribute as good role models in creative solutions. An example could be to offer reverse mentors, where younger experts teach older employees about the latest in data and the older workers convey more about management and structures. A good management team needs to make decisions based on facts but also be daring and show the way with bold decisions when required. They will also work to simplify all decisions and make visible which decisions benefit from being decentralized and empowered and which ones need to be centralized. They should also make it clear that larger changes need to be formalized, discussed, and later decided in the right decision-making forum.

When the business model is to change, it is important that the leader listens and is involved in developing a purpose for the project. Sometimes it can strengthen further with the CEO conducting an early internal seminar where the issues of the existing business are discussed and how they should handle visible bottlenecks, general value deterioration, or anything else that is of immediate concern. The executive leader needs to be able to listen and lead through others with deeper understanding in the team. An important piece of the puzzle is not to get bogged down in reactions and only pursue your own issues but to invite others into developing conversations that can later form good decision-making data. The CEO will need the help of a management team for upcoming projects, as they would of course always need them in the business regardless and get the group to set limits on the visions that the company wants to implement. Leading through others requires more clarity than ever before, more self-knowledge and humility to learn from one's own mistakes.

There are big gains in business model innovation projects to work with Three-Step Management. It is a great advantage for the project when we want to focus early on an organization, planning, and an ongoing control. In Step One, a leader of the project (often the CEO) is appointed who will lead through others with a team that analyzes, identifies, and later helps to change. The leader's task is to focus on the possibilities, keep the purpose alive, and appoint the best team for the tasks ahead, which can mean recruiting a key resource if someone is missing. In Step Two, it is primarily about the collaboration that is in focus and how the appointed team should ensure resources, motivate the leader's message, set a framework, clarify the schedule and responsibilities, and ensure that the project moves forward. Step Three involves the management appointing ambassadors who can hold the structure, answer questions, simplify the expectations, follow goals, and above all facilitate future behavioral changes. The best projects are managed on an ongoing basis but with clear guidelines for what can be implemented directly. Three-Step Management helps to save time as meetings are predetermined and the content is allowed to grow gradually.

Organizational structure

The organizational structure is a valuable element for business innovation project that relies on accessing data to create a safer and better process. The system structure often contains an overall business system that is based on a platform that has some user flexibility but changing in the direction that is usually too costly. The existing form affects the projects directly and indirectly with what is possible to plan and communicate. Therefore, it is better to see the existing system as a security and support for extracting data when planning and analyzing conditions for a project. The actual organizational structure is dependent on the business, management, and also the history of the company. The size of the company also determines how they choose to organize the implementation of the business model, whether in one solution or several.

The projects that are sketched out from various external and internal measures need to be value-enhancing and realistic. The anchoring should be broad, include planning and analysis in stages, and ensure that the implementation has a clearly harmonized message that facilitates understanding. Management needs to be observant of how the structure helps to create customer value by making bottlenecks visible in planning and later support change with ambassadors to develop new behaviors. It is important that the customer is close by and sometimes there can be great advantages to sharing important issues with the customer in an open way that develop the value. In the better companies, there are reconciliation meetings in the existing organization and before an implementation begins. The most important milestones need to be identified as to which meetings they should assessed in and when they should take place. Reconciliation meetings and milestones are central concepts to be able to follow what is improved and ensure a better organizational process.

Leaders need to be clear that they are behind the data, key figures, and the ongoing change. Information and communication are essential to be able to angle understanding from more directions and in more channels to increase the possibility that people are motivated to change behaviors. The messages should be harmonized and preferably repeated several times in different channels. If a change project contains radical changes, there need to be groups that support the project more openly and can take the lead. An alternative is to appoint early users as they can then openly try proposed changes for a period of time and then pass on their observations and learning. Communication needs to be with images, sounds, written explanations, and preferably with fixed meetings.

Variables for speed influence the way of thinking about opportunities and everything that can bring improvements regarding digitalization. It is about variables that affect the change and how they should support the strategic direction and thus the value. These can be variables that relate to the systems, quality, processes, information, communication, management, and today more and more questions about sustainability. Focusing on different processes and how they are handled in the existing systems allows for a better outcome later in the qualitative study, as the ambition is to find the processes that can be improved dynamically and contribute to a faster road. In order for a business and innovation project to be truly successful/developed/transferred to, a central system is needed along with the ability to process questions. It is important that there is a backup and trust in the existing systems that often participate or directly build the processes in the companies. For the included projects that are financially validated, a risk assessment should also be able to assess the credibility of their success.

Successful companies have analyzed the market carefully, chosen the customer area, and then checked all the key resources to be able to build their particular product or provide the market with the unique service together with others. They spend time understanding and developing the structure in line with the needs of the business model, which means good IT, modern systems, and clear agreements. The processes should be aimed at the customer's value creation with close relationships, including bringing out a need and ensuring that the entire settlement lasts from start to finish. It requires reflection, planning both overall and in detail and, above all, insights into customer needs. The leader and team must always have a focus on the business model and how it creates value for the customer. In this way, leadership is an important factor together with market knowledge.

The amount of data is a relevant question and can make it more difficult to analyze if there is simply too much. This can mean that the projects become dependent on general considerations as many variations on the same data are possible and it is important to have good preplanning.

Secondary data help the projects progress forward and serve as active support together with interviews both inside and outside the company. Collaboration between the process and system owners in the companies also needs to be highlighted. It can make a big difference to the entire project if these two variables go hand in hand where the systems support the process with facts, some brief improvements, and any tests that the company wants to do in the project.

The best projects are better planned with an extensive work to be able to analyze combinations and solve bottlenecks in ongoing business models, keeping in mind that projects often have rich data and it is a risk that it can lead to a loss of clarity. Courage to analyze and implement is critical and it is the leader together with the team and the ambassadors who execute the brave decisions by making major changes in work methodology. This often requires an understanding of why the previous behaviors were needed and encourages sensitivity to those traditions.

Resources

When a company is exposed to driving forces, it is important to map the company's resources in an inventory and determine how they affect the business model. It is an advantage if companies can have ongoing joint follow-ups of resources once a year in the overall planning. The planning that I am referring to is a set of activities that cost the company and are planned as opposed to the strategic decision early in the business model, which relates to a number of integrated opportunities in the strategy work that cannot be controlled in the same way. Not all companies have this overall planning and it is crucial that when the projects start that an inventory is made quite immediately.

Once the resource inventory is made, the company can reconcile the resources against its strategies to ensure that there are resources now but also that a lack of them does not arise later in a course correction and growth. The company can advantageously identify the most important resources in capital, HR, organizational structure, and physical resources. Next, it is crucial to classify them into four areas of quality, quantity, supply, and price. It is important that resources are focused and help the structure create value for the project. If an inventory is made carefully of all resources, together with consideration of how they relate to the model and any existing strategies, it can create other conversations and lead to cost savings later by creating deep knowledge.

When companies make their inventory of their resources and make visible what it looks like, they can try to explain whether there is contact with the existing business model and any existing strategies and exercise as necessary in its entirety. The physical products can be easier to see (e.g., any machinery) and are usually more expensive to exchange in and out from the business model. The organizational resources can be about systems that already exist and are working and can have longer agreements or point out existing collaborations that are missing. HR can be difficult to understand if a leader is lacking the experience, judgment, or loyalty to cope with the current or upcoming changes. It is important that there is pre-knowledge if the company plans to implement changes, especially within the leadership team.

There should be more interest in physical products as large investments if they are to be developed but also because there may be underlying values since owning resources in innovation projects creates a balance between the structure, people, and strategies. Business ideas and business models cannot be protected with patents or other rights but it is quite possible to create a trademark and fill it with values that chime with the idea and then it can be protected as a trademark. Product development is essential regardless because it benefits producer and consumer by focusing to create value with the customer and therefore increase growth and profit. The design can be protected as it is valuable to have exclusive rights and attract investors and to enter into sales and licensing agreements. Excellence is a competitive advantage and internal manuals with descriptions of work processes are intellectual property that can be sold or licensed. There are two clear groups regarding product innovations: those leaders who see products as a costly administrative process and those who see the process as the engine of the entire flow of innovations.

Innovation is the driver of a change project for business model innovation and it takes a very long time for companies to build in this engine so that they can control the speed themselves. The factors affecting resources and their composition will also contribute to the impact of innovation, speed, and how well a business innovation project will be successful in implementation or not. Early understanding of how resources should be used often helps development occur faster. Companies that dare to do more, are more active in their resources, and invest more in active learning also have more vibrant strategies linked to their systems and processes. The great challenge for the innovators (internal entrepreneurs), intrapreneurship, is to win the trust of the internal company.

The GUIDE

The six different themes, which I presented, can be used as a springboard for your company's journey when setting off for a business model innovation project. The 150 insights are a mix between highly detailed factors and more general approaches. The whole framework creates new opportunities for medium and large companies to build a safer and more profitable business model innovation process by using these success factors to strengthen the existing company in a business model innovation project.

GUIDE

Themes and factors

	Strategy	Existing BM	Customer orientation	Management	Organizational structure	Resource
F a c t o r s	Before	Evaluate	Energize	New situation	Security and support	Review
	Anchoring	Time	Management structure	Clarify BM	Anchored with leaders	Reinforce
	Simplify	Anchoring	Increase knowledge	Open and present	Variables for speed	Hidden values
	Load-bearing	Value	Opportunity	Lead through others	The process	Building innovations
	Living	Follow-ups	Margin and deliveries	Three-Step Management	Decision support	Implementation

Figure 8.2 A perspective of the factors within each theme of Business Model Innovation.

The ATLAS

These data are very useful in different situations, both in change and as training tool for what it can look like. The start of most projects is concentrated on which driving forces are activated, the need for the change, and later move toward what purpose a project can have in order to get the greatest possible access to primary and secondary data.

The ATLAS can support a project for innovation in its inception, in its analysis, in its planning, and in its implementation. It is extremely important that the driving forces are analyzed and that the purpose of the project has a clear basis in these driving forces. It is common for the various decision-makers to want to add their own opinions and to incorporate completely different issues, which makes a project riskier.

ATLAS

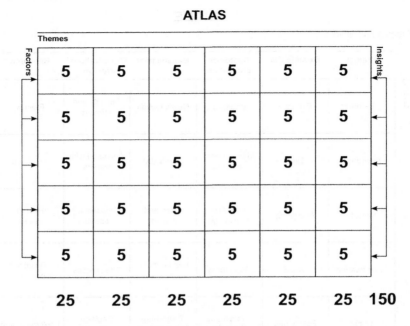

Figure 8.3 A perspective of the ATLAS containing five insights per factor leading to 150 insights.

The summary takeaways

This book is the result of three decades focused on accelerating strategies for business model innovation. It has been exciting, enriching, and at the same time demanding to follow customers' various projects. I have worked as an action researcher, followed customers closely, and over time developed knowledge about the processes of change. For me, it has meant participating in entire transitions, doing partial analyses, and/or being a mentor to companies that need innovation of their business model.

An early insight was to separate the project and the ongoing operations until there was a decision with a plan for what was to be developed and improved where there are more costs involved. The early improvements can create good results that can be crucial later on to improve the business. It is about companies needing to spend more time on their issues for growth and scale their businesses in smarter ways.

A further insight is that most companies do not have well-thought-out business models as a whole, but that the conversation is often around strategies, different deals, and the best organizational solution. It has changed as the term has become more common, but I feel that developing business models is used more in smaller companies and in the technology sector than in the largest industries.

It is also important to mention the different conditions for creating a project and to acknowledge that knowledge is as diverse as people are. Sometimes management may feel that IT systems should be able to deliver more, while there is a view of administrative processes as costly. I have worked with many ERP systems and have been involved in an incredible number of implementations of different sizes. The increased awareness and use of ChatGPT and other technologies has many exciting possibilities in the field of business model innovation. While it is possible, if not likely, for several fields to experience a reduction in staffing requirements, such as customer service and banking, there will also be an increase in roles to ensure that the technology is working as it should and provide a backup in case of system failure. In this brave new technological world, this new framework provides a great opportunity for medium and large companies to implement change with innovation more successfully.

The last years with COVID-19 have opened up the world of work to allow the work environment to be more flexible, which includes allowing workers to be able to work in a hybrid way (from home and in the office) and many have also continued to exclusively work from home. I have noticed that company management believes that the systems can handle hybrid work; that people should report everything from experiences; and that the systems can access solutions, project time, and deviations. However, many companies also believe that consensus is partially lost when people do not meet in person and therefore it can be difficult to get the voice as the only part of the communication through phone meetings and e-mail. I can find validity in both approaches; the structure can be the shell and the knowledge content no matter where you are.

Those who have read this far clearly have the adventurer's spirit that I have had the pleasure of witnessing over the past 25 years of working with medium and large companies on an international scale. Change is never easy and it can be daunting even to the strongest leaders. However, it is those who dare and who are willing to take the risk and ask the questions who often gain the greatest outcomes for their companies. It is true that there have been times where the final decisions have led to taking things back to the very basics when working with an organization, but from taking such a drastic step, new and exciting projects have come about, which in the end served the company, market, and customer better than anything that existed before. The wealth of experience I have gained from all of the people I have interviewed, the seminars I have led, the CEOs I have worked with, and all those who have been a part of the change projects I have worked on has come down to this – a book that begins to outline this new frontier of change in business strategy and business model innovation.

The reality is that in this day and age, more than ever before, the world of work is evolving and changing at an increasingly accelerated pace. While the traditional wisdom and ways of working should be acknowledged and appreciated for bringing us to the present moment, it is clear that more is needed if individual companies, markets, and even industries are going to survive going into the future. Having knowledge in itself is not enough; progress forward requires vision paired with insight that is informed, clear, and inclusive.

In this way, this book shows how it works, takes the practice of business model innovation out of the world of theory, and energizes innovation by providing a series of themes, factors, and insights that can propel a company into action. This action takes the form of looking at a business with a lens of honesty, in seeing the reality of the current business position and then identifying the steps forward to meaningful and lasting growth. The world of business in the twenty-first century is not a solid and stagnant thing; it is dynamic and constantly evolving in an ever-changing world. It is not enough for a business to innovate; it must be brave enough to consistently take on a journey, an adventure, of change.

ATLAS, 150 insights

Strategy

Before
- Clarify role for implementation
- Understand behaviors from existing business model (resistance)
- Inventory of the existing strategies
- Understand the personal issues (work, home, and leisure)
- Improve with review and trimming

Anchoring
- Create space for understanding
- Refine, evaluate, and plan future strategies
- Major changes require other strategies
- Support from decision-makers
- Managers needs to have self-control qualities

Simplify
- Develop short, clear, and logical strategies
- Possible to communicate to justify the change
- Good beginning and clear ends
- Understanding should be responsible, measurable, and completed
- Work with number to justify the implementation (important)

Load-bearing
- Stronger if signal a value
- Stronger if they are empathic
- Carrying, leading, and communicative
- Target images works very well: vision
- Effectiveness mapped against existing business model

Living
- Larger projects in larger organizations
- Capture attention, highlights, and reinforces a company
- Should describe daily activities
- Should be used tighter, more focused, and prioritized
- Helpful between generations and diversified companies

Figure 8.4 Factors and insights in strategy.

Existing business model

Evaluate
- Acknowledge ignorance and where understanding differs
- Reconciliations are important for creating value
- Identifications of early agreements, inventory
- Management must be informed about old agreements
- Identify central behaviors around central decisions for the model

Time
- Understanding and ensuring the accuracy of the needs
- Internal time for review of the business model
- Map the value created in customer relationships
- Creative process that requires planning, mapping, and time
- Management often determines the conditions (step back)

Anchoring
- Business model and how customer value is created
- Faster access to fact-based decisions
- Increased insight into the development of customer value
- Local anchoring in international companies is important
- Social process between owners, board, and management

Value
- Deepening their understanding of customer behavior
- Clear customer value benefit to a better process
- Search for unique value
- Make a general inventory of the value
- Use test of value from throughout the value chain

Follow-ups
- Inventory of all communications and behaviors
- Planning of information and communication channels
- Analyzed and developed customer value
- Unified message with images, sounds, and written words
- Regular follow-up meetings with customers

Figure 8.5 Factors and insights in existing business model.

Customer orientation

Energize
- Secure an international outlook
- Inventory of external driving forces
- Follow and inventory of customer groups
- Identify future valuable needs and customer management
- Develop new values over already-existing values

Management structure
- Work proactively with a customer manager
- Follow early process of value creation, inventory
- Build important relationships in carefully selected segments
- Deepen knowledge of the current business model
- Set a marketing strategy for innovation projects

Increase knowledge
- Acquire knowledge through activity
- Follow consumers volatile and unfaithful to brands
- Reverse mentorship with younger groups
- Search for trends, driving forces, and skills in other countries
- Distribution of resources and values for reducing risks

Opportunity
- Thoughtful, detailed, and focused strategies
- Think bigger, add value without losing sight in reality
- Focus on customer behavior and access to key resources
- Alternative solutions and offers support for change
- Prioritize value-creating activities

Margin and deliveries
- Describe real customer value without uncertainty
- Explain the agreed margins customer prepared to pay
- Predetermine prices with facts and experience
- Open processes, communication, and world-class deliveries
- Focus on deliveries from start to finish

Figure 8.6 Factors and insights in customer orientation.

Management

New situation
- Control of managers insight, and knowledge from start
- CEO included in the decision-making in the project
- Handle past legacy from leaders more openly
- Focus on future valuable needs
- Secure the purpose and intent of the project with anchoring

Clarify BM
- Stand behind the decisions, messages, and behaviors
- Lead by example of time and acting with care
- Identify bottlenecks and behaviors
- Increase creativity and better values
- Use success factors as a mirror for possible implementations

Open and present
- Work for an open solution with freer approach
- Offer extended openness for fact to create better decisions
- Offer technology mentors to speed new knowledge
- Give confidence in creativity, proximity, and be brave
- What can be decentralized and centralized

Lead through others
- Clarifying the purpose of the project
- Seminar to analyze more and implement the project
- Listen and lead the way through deeper understanding
- Inventory of important attributes through leadership team
- Different levels of management secure support

Three-Step Management
- Focus on the organization, planning and ongoing control
- Step 1 is to appoint a leader for the project
- Step 2 is to focus on collaboration with the team
- Step 3 is to secure ambassadors
- Save time, meetings are predetermined, and content grow gradually

Figure 8.7 Factors and insights in management.

Organizational structure

Security and support
- Support from systems for a safer process
- Inventory to understand the structure (in – not change)
- Explain the projects use of the structure
- Focus on the important data that can bring value
- Look for flexibility and user-friendly solutions

Anchored with leaders
- The team present a value-creation plan, including ambassador
- Secure the effects on the structure, inventory
- Reconciliation and important milestones, plan seminars
- Communication plan with overall message
- Radical changes, create social groups for implementation

Variables for speed
- Influence the way of thinking about opportunities (inventory)
- Focus on different processes for a better outcome (search)
- Develop central system and process questions
- Backup and trust in the existing systems
- Make a risk assessment (credibility)

The process
- Learn from the company's customer process (market, segment, and value)
- Create a strength and weakness analysis of the structure
- Directing the process toward the customer
- Describe an overall process, including details and insight
- The management needs to secure the value creation

Decision support
- Secure good preplanning of the data
- Primary and secondary data work good together
- Focus on collaboration between the process and system owners
- Plan and solve bottlenecks in ongoing business models (rich data risk)
- Trust the data and be brave and bold

Figure 8.8 Factors and insights in organizational structure.

Resource

Review
- Make an early inventory of all resources
- Update resources ongoing (list once a year)
- Go through the existing business model
- Resources in four categories (human, capital, structure, and physical)
- Use the structure for value creation (dominant resources)

Reinforce
- Create deep knowledge for potential cost savings
- Search for contact with or within the existing business model
- Search for physicals (more expensive with more potential)
- Make an inventory of the intangible assets (organizational)
- Go through the human resources (search for potential strengths)

Hidden values
- Search for underlaying values in physical products
- Fill the trademark with value (potential to register)
- Focus on unique product development (potential profit)
- The design can be valuable
- Search for intellectual property

Building innovations
- Innovation is the engine of a change, plan for control
- Early understanding of resources develops faster
- Invest more time in resources and get quicker return
- The intrapreneurs need to win the internal trust
- Invest more time and build more active knowledge

Implementation
- Leadership that works through others (Three-Step Management)
- Clear way, which parts need to be improved and later implemented
- Anchored and having a clear purpose
- Detailed description but few are centralized
- Be bold, allocate time and resources

Figure 8.9 Factors and insights in resources.

Business Model Innovation
How it really works

ATLAS

6 Themes, 30 Factors, 150 Insights

Pages

1. Front page
2. Explanation
3. Strategy
4. Existing business model
5. Customer orientation
6. Management
7. Organizational structure
8. Resources
9. Important questions
10. Summary
11. GUIDE
12. Back page

Collect your digital companion brochure from
www.cecia.se

Figure 8.10 Business Model Innovation e-brochure, available from Cecia Consulting.

Index

5G 109

Alpha 27, 116, 132
anchor 42, 78, 156
anchoring 8, 16, 20, 45, 82, 106, 108, 119, 128, 131, 138

before 12, 16, 27
Bretton Woods 7, 128
business model innovation ATLAS 2, 4, 8, 149, 150, 165, 166, 169
business model innovation GUIDE 2, 3, 4, 149, 150, 164

Cecia Consulting 1, 11, 175
ChatGPT 42, 132, 133, 167
common forms 101; division 101; flat 101; function 101; matrix 101
COVID-19 15, 18, 57, 60, 61, 67, 77, 86, 104, 113, 167
CRM 47, 56, 120
C-suites 1, 160
customer orientation 3, 46, 56, 61, 75, 157, 158, 171

decision support 116, 120

energizing 3, 56, 68
ERP 102
existing business model 3, 9, 16, 29, 34, 38, 130, 138, 148, 155

First World War 5, 20

General Agreement on Tariffs and Trade (GATT) 38

Generations Z 133
global international groups 1

hidden values 3, 132, 136, 145
hybrid work 57, 61, 86, 167

insights 2, 4, 5, 151, 166
International Monetary Fund 7
Internet 5, 6, 24, 117
Iron Curtain 5

leading through others 82, 90, 93, 116, 141, 154, 160
living strategies 3, 27, 28, 29, 30, 32, 152, 155
load-bearing 24, 27

main areas of resources 125; capital 124, 133, 140; human 125, 127; physical 125, 128; structure 125, 128
management 3, 8, 10, 18, 37, 38, 41, 45, 60, 63, 78, 79, 80, 82, 85, 94, 97, 146, 159, 169, 172
mirror 3, 51, 85, 146, 169

online analytical processing (OLAP) 117
organizational structure 3, 41, 101, 103, 105, 107, 108, 114, 120, 121, 126, 152, 161, 163, 173
Organization for Economic Cooperation and Development (OECD) 38
Organization for European Economic Co-operation (OEEC) 38

original equipment manufacturers
(OEM) 133

resources 3, 8, 11, 17, 40, 43, 47, 58,
66, 67, 81, 93, 124, 128, 132,
140, 153, 163, 172, 174

search engine optimization (SEO) 47
Sea Road 5
Second World War 12, 20, 128
selected cases 2, 10
Silk Road 5
simplify 20, 24
social media 6, 117
strategy 3, 12, 24, 128, 153
structure perplexity 2, 109, 110, 152

success factors 2, 3, 4, 5, 9, 85, 148,
152, 164, 172

themes 2, 3, 9, 10, 58, 148, 149, 150,
151, 164, 168
Three-Step Management 3, 8, 93, 94,
95, 97, 99, 117, 141, 143, 144,
152, 160, 161, 165, 172, 174

values 8, 24, 48, 59, 88, 136, 158, 164
variables for speed 3, 108, 112, 122,
152, 162

World Bank 7
World War II 7, 12
WTO 5, 38, 129

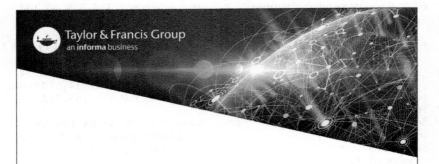